Business Plans for Small Businesses

How to prepare, write and pitch a successful business plan

Colin Barrow

*Business Plans for Small Businesses: How to prepare, write and pitch
a successful business plan*

This first edition published in 2012 by Crimson Publishing Ltd., Westminster House, Kew
Road, Richmond, Surrey TW9 2ND

Author: Colin Barrow

British Library Cataloguing in Publication Data
A catalogue record for this book is available from the British Library

ISBN 978 1 85458 684 1

Typeset by IDSUK (DataConnection) Ltd
Printed and bound in Great Britain by TJ International Ltd, Padstow, Cornwall

Contents

Contents

Contents

Contents

Introduction

How often do you succumb to an envious glance at a successful entrepreneur, assigning their success more to luck than judgement? Bill Gates was lucky to come in at the start of the boom in demand for personal computers; Steve Jobs just hitched a ride on Sony's Walkman trajectory as it burnt out; Google's founders came in at a fortuitous moment after Tim Berners-Lee had done all the hard brainwork in getting the internet off the ground; Facebook's founder Mark Zuckerberg arrived on the scene as social networks were becoming the rage.

Difficult as it may be to believe, people actually make their own luck. "The harder I practice the luckier I get." This quote, attributed to former world champion golfer Gary Player, is perhaps a more realistic view of how great performers get to be great. Player is the only golfer in the 20th century to have won the British Open in three different decades – so he knows something about being in it for the long haul.

Practice, as they say, makes perfect.

Preparing a business plan is in effect a practice run at shaping up your strategy to start, grow or redirect a business venture. Indeed, it is a chance to make your mistakes on paper before you go to market.

In today's unforgiving environment we need all the luck we can get. With the margin for error shrinking and financial institutions getting even more picky over who they will support, the key differentiator for anyone looking in on a business from the outside is the business plan.

Yes, it will take time to prepare and write it, but this is important, and ultimately rewarding, work. This book will show you how.

Startups Tip

Doing a business plan isn't as hard as you might think. You don't have to write a doctoral thesis or a novel. This book will guide you through the process and Startups.co.uk has valuable pointers as well as links to software available to provide you with a workable template.

↪ CHAPTER 1

Understanding business planning

📖 What's in this chapter?

You could be forgiven for thinking that having a business plan is one luxury you can do without. After all, most people who start a business don't have a business plan, and many of those that do don't commit it to paper. But as most new businesses fail, following the herd may not be such a great idea! While having a business plan won't necessarily make your business fly, it will greatly reduce the chance of hitting foreseeable problems before you get off the ground.

In this chapter we'll cover:

↪ what exactly is a business plan and what do we mean by it?

↪ who is it for?

↪ what if you don't plan?

↪ the key components of a business plan

↪ how long should it be and how far ahead should you plan?

↪ establishing credibility.

What exactly is a business plan and what do we mean by it?

Business plans can mean very different things to different people.

Some business starters, the majority according to many researchers of the field, have no plan. For them any road will take them to where they are going. Often their road is short: well over two-thirds of new businesses close down before they reach their second year. Some consider it more of a concept than a road map. For them business is an unfolding adventure only to be revealed as time goes by. After all, they claim, no one really knows what is going to happen tomorrow with much certainty. So why bother putting a lot of effort into trying to guess what might happen a year or so in the future? For them a business plan is a little more than a statement of intent. Phrases such as "We are going to make and sell greetings cards" or "I will open my own restaurant" are enough to get their show on the road.

For others, particularly those who like numbers, a business plan is a spreadsheet, or better still several spreadsheets, full of detailed projections covering sales, costs and anything else that can be shown in figures far into the distant future.

Defining the business plan

A business plan is a written statement setting out what you want to achieve, the way you expect to realise your goals and why you believe they are attainable. It should also spell out the resources in terms of finance, equipment, premises and people that you will need. As well as outlining the structure of your business, the product or service and the customer, your business plan should also show in what way your proposition will be different from what is already on the market.

As well as giving information about your business, your business plan should also inspire you and any backers that your business has growth potential and you have the ability to get the business underway successfully. While it's a blueprint for what you want to achieve, and should give you a clear understanding of how you intend to get there, it's not in any way a rigid prediction of every future occurrence. You can't control the future, and outside circumstances will have an effect on the shape and direction of your business. But a good business plan should at least give you a clear direction to aim for, and the means to assess progress towards the achievement of objectives.

For anyone already in business, the starting point of your plan is an explanation of where you are now and what you have already achieved in terms of sales revenues and profits.

What do we mean by a business plan?

While a business plan is statement of what you plan to achieve, your readers are more likely to be interested in the thought process that led you to its contents, and to the assumptions that underpin it, than in the detail of the plan itself. That's not in any way to devalue your writing, it's just that your readers, whether bankers, prospective partners – or even friends and relatives – know that things rarely turn out exactly as planned.

The explanation as to how you arrive at a particular conclusion will often be more important than the conclusion itself. For example, let's suppose that you have put in £120,000 as your first year's sales goal. A business plan that shows £12,000 a month sales from the outset will lack any credibility. Anyone with real-life business experience will know that it takes time to pick up business. A plan that shows sales growing over time, supported by a clear explanation of how they will be achieved, is much more believable than one that is arrived at by dividing a figure by 12. So if sales will come from generating enquiries, and enquiries come from advertising, you need to support your goal with the relationship you expect between these events. So, for example, if your adverts can be expected on average to generate 100 enquiries, which will produce eight orders worth £1,000 each, you will be demonstrating the thought that has gone into your planning.

A business plan, then, is much more than the written document itself. It's the sum of all the thinking, research and experience that has gone into the process behind putting the plan together. But don't worry if you don't have much by way of business planning process now. That, after all, is what this book is about.

startups | **Business Plans for Small Businesses**

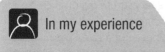 In my experience

Simon Woodroffe, YO! Sushi

"It took two very full years from having my start-up idea to the first day's trading."

Who is your business plan for?

As a general rule, entrepreneurs wisely want to keep the business model at the heart of their business plan a secret. But, with that in mind, they are in danger of writing as though they will be the main, perhaps even the only, reader.

JARGON BUSTER

Business model is a buzzword made popular in the great dotcom bubble era of 1999–2000: it explains how a business will generate revenue.

Unless you intend to start up on your own, using your own money, you should write your business plan with other readers in mind. There are ways to limit the danger of your business idea from being ripped off by anyone reading your business plan – using a non-disclosure agreement (NDA), for example.

JARGON BUSTER

Non-disclosure agreements are confidentiality agreements that bind recipients to maintain your 'secrets' and not to take any action that could damage the value of that 'secret'. This means that they can't share the information with anyone else or act on the idea themselves, for a period of time at least.

> **Startups Tip**
> You can use NDAs with potential clients, suppliers, advisors, investors or even employees if you have to share confidential information that could threaten the success of your venture if it fell into the wrong hands.

A business plan is not a 'one size fits all' document, so the more it appears to have been written specifically for a particular reader the more likely they are to read it and have empathy with the contents.

Below are some of the people you may want to show your business plan to, and some ideas on how you should tweak the contents to meet their needs. You don't have to write completely different business plans for different types of reader. Just include (or limit) certain pieces of information, emphasise some parts more and perhaps change the running order. Remember, you have to be able to justify every line of your business plan and the thinking behind it. So expect your readers to probe; the style of presentation is just to capture their attention in the first place.

> **Startups Tip**
> Think about who your audience will be and the information they will need before starting to research your business plan. A bank manager, business angel or venture capitalist will all be poring over your business plan in great detail before they risk putting their money into it.

The main audiences for your business plan are described below.

Your bank manager

Bankers (and indeed anyone lending you money) are looking for some form of asset security to back their loan – usually a property such as the family home. They also want the near certainty of getting their money back, so they don't want to hear too much about meteoric growth prospects; that usually just means pumping in more cash before the business becomes profitable. They will also want to charge an interest rate that reflects current market conditions and their view of the level of risk of the proposal. That in turn means bankers will usually expect a business to start repaying both the loan and the interest on a monthly or quarterly basis immediately after the loan has been granted. Bankers also hope the business will succeed so that they can lend more money in the future and provide more banking services such as insurance and tax advice to a loyal customer.

Investors

Investors don't expect a new business to have many assets so they are up for taking a risk. But because the inherent risks involved in investing in new and young ventures are greater than for investing in established companies, their investors expect the chance of larger overall returns. To do that, fund managers must not only keep failures to a minimum; they have to pick some big winners too – ventures with annual compound growth rates above 50% – to offset the inevitable mediocre performers. Typically, a fund manager would expect, from any 10 investments, one star, seven also-rans and two flops.

It is important to remember that, despite this outcome, venture capital fund managers are only looking for winners. So to appeal to this audience, your plan needs to emphasise the prospects of fast growth and big returns. They will expect you to recruit a team of great people, shell out for patents and be cash hungry for a year or two. Not only are venture capitalists looking for winners, they are also looking for a substantial shareholding in your business. You have to be forming a company from the outset and show that you understand that having 70% of a big business is worth a lot more than a 100% share in a small one.

> ### Startups Tip
> If you're putting together a business plan to raise funding, the plan becomes even more critical in determining the success or failure of your business. "It is the initial selling document and it will either get you in the door or not," according to Paul Murray of Europe's largest venture capital firm 3i.

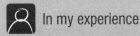

In my experience

Sophie Cornish, Notonthehighstreet.com

"If you can find a business partner with complementary skills, that's 90% of the work done."

Key employees or partners

When anyone in this audience reads your business plan they want to hear about unlimited growth prospects and exciting opportunities, all to be realised taking very little (or better still no) risk. If the employee you want to recruit is leaving a good job to join you, there is usually a reason. Often they just want the opportunity for recognition or career progression. While a banker may consider creating a management position as an unnecessary overhead for a young business, you will need them if you are to grow. Your business plan is a good way to show how, when the business achieves its goals, there will be opportunities for promotion.

Partners share some of the characteristics of employees, but in particular they will want to read about the opportunity to own a part of a worthwhile venture, perhaps also being able to build on that stake as the firm grows.

In my experience

Mary and Doug Perkins, Specsavers

"Our entire business plan was based on getting professional opticians to buy into our proposition. Back in 1984 we realised that for opticians to really feel part of their business, they had to have a stake in its ownership and profits. As a result we built a joint venture partnership model in which opticians share ownership of their stores on a 50:50 basis with our company. They have to put up half the money to get their shop off the ground. We believe opticians will work much harder and deliver top-notch customer service as an entrepreneur running their own business rather than as an employee."

Sanity check

That's not to imply that anyone starting a business or planning to grow their business is in any way mad; what would be foolish is to embark on it without a business plan. Preparing a business plan is essential if you are to both focus your ideas and test your resolve about entering or expanding your business. It is also a chance to make your mistakes on paper rather than in the marketplace. One would-be business starter on a programme at Cranfield found that the price he proposed to charge would never be sufficient to recover his overheads or break-even, two terms he hadn't come across before starting to write up his business plan!

Once completed, your business plan will serve as a blueprint to follow, which, like any map, improves the user's chances of reaching the destination.

JARGON BUSTER

Overheads are the costs that a business incurs in order to be able to trade. Buying or renting premises, acquiring machinery or equipment and setting up a website, for example.

Despite the obvious benefits, thousands of would-be entrepreneurs still attempt to start without a business plan. The most common among these are businesses that either appear to need little or no capital at the outset, or whose founders have funds of their own. In both cases it is believed unnecessary to expose the project to harsh financial appraisal. The former hypothesis is usually based on the easily exploded myth that customers will all pay cash on the nail and suppliers will wait for months to be paid. In the meantime, the proprietor has the use of these funds to finance the business. Such model customers and suppliers are thinner on the ground than optimistic entrepreneurs think.

In any event, two important market rules still apply: either the product or service on offer fails to sell like hot cakes and mountains of unpaid stocks build up, all of which eventually have to be financed; or it does sell like hot cakes and more financially robust entrepreneurs are attracted into the market. Without the staying power that adequate financing provides, these new competitors will rapidly kill off the entrepreneur.

JARGON BUSTER

When all costs have been covered from the revenue made by selling goods and services a business has reached break-even.

Those would-be entrepreneurs with funds of their own, or worse still with funds borrowed from 'innocent' friends and relatives, tend to think that the time spent in preparing a business plan could be more usefully (and enjoyably) spent looking for premises, buying a new car or installing a computer. In short, anything that inhibits them from immediate action is viewed as time-wasting. As most people's perception of their business venture is flawed in some important respect, it follows that jumping in at the deep end is risky – and unnecessarily so.

Flaws can often be discovered cheaply and in advance when preparing a business plan; they are always discovered in the marketplace, invariably at a much higher and usually fatal cost.

There was a myth at the start of the internet boom that the pace of development in the sector was too fast for business planning. The first generation of dotcom businesses and their backers seemed happy to pump money into what they called 'killer applications'. These were little more than brief statements of intent supported with wishful thinking. Now only ventures with a well-prepared business plan have any chance of getting off the ground or being supported in later stage financing rounds.

In my experience

Nick Jenkins, Moonpig

"Whilst at Cranfield taking an MBA, I researched different business models carefully. I wanted to take an existing product and somehow transform and improve it using the internet and existing technology. Thinking my business proposition through thoroughly before launching out into business helped me rule out a number of possibilities and made sure I was confident in the model I had chosen."

What if you don't plan? What successful entrepreneurs have to say about the value of having a business plan

Luckily for entrepreneurs, having a business plan is more or less compulsory if you want to raise money, recruit great staff or pull in a partner. But don't just take our word for it. Johnnie Boden's business struggled for the first three years on its journey from bedroom to boardroom through a near catastrophic lack of capital. "We kept on running out of cash," says Boden. "Although the concept was strong, I had no decent business plan." Although in his own words Boden did not have a "swanky start-up" he did invest £300,000 early on. With hindsight, perhaps that could have been delivered by having a business plan; his business really needed double that sum to have less of a roller-coaster ride in the early years.

Startups Tip

Too many businesses make business plans only when they have no choice in the matter. Unless the bank or the investors want a plan, there is no plan. Don't wait to write your plan until you think you'll have enough time. "I can't plan. I'm too busy getting things done," business people say. The busier you are, the more you need to plan.

The key components of a business plan

While there is no such thing as a 'universal' business plan format, certain layouts and contents seem to have been more successful for entrepreneurs than others. Here are some guidelines to producing an attractive business plan, from both an owner's and a financier's perspective.

Cover and table of contents

First, the cover should show the name of the business, the date on which the plan was prepared and your name, addresses (including email and website), phone number and mobile number. Anyone reading the business plan may want to talk over some aspects of the proposal before arranging a meeting.

Having written the business plan you will know exactly where everything in it is, but any other reader needs some pointers to guide them through the maze: that's what the table of contents does. Number each main section, marketing, finance, people and so forth 1,2,3; important elements within a section can then be designated 1.1, 1.2 and so on.

Executive summary

This is the most important part of your plan and will form the heart of your 'elevator pitch' (see Chapter 16 for more on this). Written last, this should be punchy, short (ideally one page but never more than two), and should enthuse any reader. Its primary purpose is to get an outsider – bank manager, business angel or prospective partner – to want to read the rest of the business plan. It should include the following.

- What your product/service is and why it's different from what is around now and why customers need what you plan to offer.
- How close you are to being ready to sell your product/service and what if anything remains to be done in terms of development, sourcing materials, finding premises and getting equipped.

- Why you have the skills and expertise to start up and run this business; who else you need to help in your business (and how you will recruit them).
- Financial projections showing how much money you need to start up and operate for the first year or so; if you don't have sufficient money, how much will you need to raise and what security can you offer to a lender, or shareholding for an investor?
- How you will operate your business. Sketch out the key steps from buying in any raw materials, through to selling, delivering and getting paid.

The contents: putting flesh on the bones

Unlike the executive summary that is structured to reveal the essence of your business proposition, the plan itself should follow a logical sequence such as the one below.

- *Marketing:* includes information on the product/service on offer, customers and the size of the market, competitors, proposed pricing, promotion and selling and distribution methods.
- *Operations:* includes information on any processes such as manufacture, assembly, purchasing, stock holding, delivery/fulfilment and website.
- *Financial projections:* includes information on sales and cashflow for the next 12–18 months, showing how much money is needed, for what and by when.
- *Premises:* includes the space and equipment that will be needed.
- *People:* the skills and experience you have that will help you run this business; the other people you will need and where you will find them.
- *Administrative matters:* includes any intellectual property (IP) on your product or service that you might have. What insurance will you need? What bookkeeping and accounting system will you use? How will you keep customer, supplier and employee records?
- *Milestone timetable:* this should show the key actions you have still to take to be ready to sell your product or service, and the date these will be completed.
- *Appendices:* use these for any bulky information such as market studies, competitors' leaflets, customer endorsements, technical data, patents and CVs that you refer to in your business plan.
- *Glossary:* includes definitions of any technical or industry-specific terms that you have used.

How long should it be and how far ahead should you plan?

There are two areas that are the subject of much debate among professional business plan readers, and writers for that matter: how long should the business plan be and how far ahead should you plan?

Length

There is a definite consensus that less is more when it comes to business plans. You should resist the temptation to embark on *War and Peace* and think more along the lines of a snappy short story. Twenty pages should be enough, and you can always use an appendix for any large amounts of data. Cranfield students have entered and won awards in many annual business plan contests over the years with the finalists never using fewer than 20 pages or more than 50 pages. At the end of the day, readability matters more than page count.

Format, layout, headings and white spaces all bulk out the text but they make the words themselves easier to digest. Using charts to point up numbers makes projections easier to grasp. Photographs, illustrations and drawings can bring products, locations and equipment to life in ways that can rarely be achieved with words alone. But these visual elements soak up pages.

The acid test is that a great business plan should leave a reader with a sound appreciation of your business after a quick browse, soaking in the main points in no more than 15 minutes.

> **Startups Tip**
> Keep your plan short. Around 30 pages is more than long enough to explain most ventures.

Distance

Back in 1967, the Long Range Planning Society (LRP) was founded to foster a better understanding of how businesses could plan more effectively. Then the vogue was for a five- to seven-year planning horizon, with some enthusiasts championing a stretch to 10, 15 and even 25 years. Today the LRP has changed its name to the Strategic Planning Society, and businesses have shrunk the scope of their business plans to a more modest three to five years.

There are no hard and fast rules on how far into the future your business plan should look, but any investor would expect to see you project out to the point where your venture is making a profit, or at least is cashflow positive (see Chapter 10 for more on this).

Establishing credibility

Unless you are already in business and are preparing a business plan for a successful venture with a sound trading history, you are likely to have a credibility gap. Your reader has only you and your business plan to use as a measure as to your chance of success.

> **Startups Tip**
>
> Don't overestimate the importance of the idea. You don't need a great idea to start a business; you need time, money, perseverance and common sense. Few successful businesses are based entirely on new ideas. A new idea is harder to sell than an existing one, because often people don't understand a new idea and they are often unsure if it will work. Plans don't sell new business ideas to investors. People do. Investors invest in people, not ideas. The plan, although necessary, is only a way to present information.

Track record

Your business plan is the main and perhaps only opportunity you will get to set out your track record of achievements that relate to the venture you are putting forward. This is not about trawling out a selection of school prizes and education certificates, though in moderation these are helpful. Don't worry too much if your academic record is less than distinguished. After all Sir Richard Branson (Virgin) dropped out of full-time education at 16, and Lord Sugar (Amstrad), Sir Philip Green (BHS and Arcadia, the group that includes Topshop and Miss Selfridge), Sir Bernie Ecclestone (Formula One) and Charles Dunstone (Carphone Warehouse) all gave higher education a miss.

Gender and age don't count for much either. More than a third of new businesses are started by women, and those over 55 are as likely to be writing their first business plan as youngsters fresh out of school. Furniture company IKEA was founded by Ingvar Kamprad when he was just 17, having cut his teeth on selling matches to his nearby neighbours at the age of five, followed by a spell selling flower seeds, greeting cards, Christmas decorations and eventually furniture. The key attributes to bring to the fore are your ability to deliver results, ideally in or around the field of business you are planning to enter or expand in.

In my experience

Edwina Dunn and Clive Humby, dunnhumby

"We wrote a good business plan; we'd been well trained in our previous company, CACI a market analysis company that used census data to predict consumer lifestyle patterns. Using our industry experience we presented our business plan to Geoffrey Squire, CEO of Oracle UK at the time and an angel investor. We knew his backing would be easier to secure as he knew us on a personal level and was aware of our track record."

Business viability

Your business plan is the vehicle to prove to you and to others that your ideas are soundly based. If your business idea is based on a novel and as yet unproven idea – a description that fits only a very small number of ventures – then your plan has to focus on the customer need your product or service will meet. The iPad is perhaps the most visible example of an innovative product for which there was no obvious need. However, Apple does have a large, affluent customer base of people who like to see themselves as sector trendsetters: that is the real need being met.

It is more likely that you will be entering a market with well-entrenched competitors. Fortunately, being first into a market is not all that it's cracked up to be. According to research, over half of businesses that were first into their markets are destined to fail. What is more important is that you use your business plan to demonstrate what you have learnt from the current players and how your proposition will be different. We look in detail at this area in Chapter 5.

In my experience

Richard Reed, innocent

"Every time someone said 'No' I just said 'Why not?' They'd say 'It won't work', I'd say 'Why not?' They'd say 'It's too expensive', we'd say 'We know there's people who will pay it'. It's a case of overcoming each hurdle at a time."

Checklist

☑ Have you written your business plan as your real-life guide for getting your business off the ground, not just to keep the bank happy?

☑ Allow enough time for research. A well thought through business plan can take months, even on occasion years, to put together.

☑ Have you included all the essential information, ideally in summary form so not to overload your readers with too much detail?

☑ Make sure you include any relevant past experience that can demonstrate your suitability to start this business.

↶ CHAPTER 2
Market research

📖 What's in this chapter?

Understanding the structure and forces at work in your market is the starting point for any successful business planning process. Ask any banker or venture capital provider how much you need to know about your market and the answer, however unhelpful it may sound, will be 'everything'. What they really mean is that you should demonstrate in your plan that you have a sound appreciation of the forces that drive your industry. Although every business (and the industry in which it operates) is different in some respect, the framework for analysis is reasonably standard.

In this chapter we'll cover:

→ *reviewing the big picture*
→ *establishing your knowledge gaps*
→ *the tools of the trade*

→ desk and field research
→ using the internet
→ doing surveys online
→ testing the market
→ understanding the data.

Reviewing the big picture

The purpose of market research is to ensure you have sufficient information on customers, competitors and markets, so that you can be reasonably confident that people will want to buy what you want to sell at a price that will give you a viable business proposition. You do not have to start a business, launch a new product or enter a market to prove there are no customers for your goods or services; frequently, even some modest market research beforehand can give clear guidance as to how tough it will be to carve out a space for you to operate in.

Suppose you are planning to start a business baking and selling organic bread. Using only the freshest ingredients, you aim to create good-quality breads and challenge the idea that bread is bad for us. Your plan is to use a traditional baking method taking it slow and letting the dough rise and prove naturally at its own speed to enable the full flavour of the dough to develop.

Certainly sounds good enough to eat, but is it worth backing? The founder of this seemingly simple business is about to enter an industry that doesn't take it slow: in fact, it takes no prisoners.

Michael Porter, a seriously clever Harvard Business School professor, has developed a process called 'The Five Forces Theory of Industry Analysis'. Despite sounding like business school speak, this is a useful tool for getting an overview of the areas any business plan must get a handle on to be taken seriously.

> ### Startups Tip
> Even if you don't want to raise money for your business now, having a well-researched business plan will stand you in good stead if and when you do. The quality of your market research may just be the factor that tips a financing decision in your favour. Look on high-grade research as an important asset that can act as bank or investor collateral.

We will look in Chapter 6 at how to use our understanding of those forces to shape our strategy, but here we first have to get an appreciation of the forces and then see how to research our market to get answers to the questions posed. We will use our organic baker as an example to bring the forces into sharper focus.

Supplier power

The fewer the suppliers, the more powerful they usually are. Oil is a classic example where fewer than a dozen countries supply the whole world market and consequently can set prices. Our baker's proposition also looks like a supplier-dominated sector. Organic bread uses only four ingredients to make the basic dough: flour, fresh yeast, water

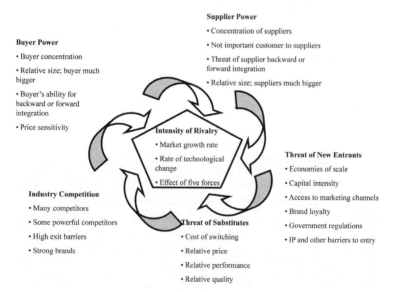

Supplier Power
• Concentration of suppliers
• Not important customer to suppliers
• Threat of supplier backward or forward integration
• Relative size; suppliers much bigger

Buyer Power
• Buyer concentration
• Relative size; buyer much bigger
• Buyer's ability for backward or forward integration
• Price sensitivity

Intensity of Rivalry
• Market growth rate
• Rate of technological change
• Effect of five forces

Threat of New Entrants
• Economies of scale
• Capital intensity
• Access to marketing channels
• Brand loyalty
• Government regulations
• IP and other barriers to entry

Industry Competition
• Many competitors
• Some powerful competitors
• High exit barriers
• Strong brands

Threat of Substitutes
• Cost of switching
• Relative price
• Relative performance
• Relative quality

Figure 2.1 Five forces theory of industry analysis

and salt (with power as the remaining 'ingredient'). There are few suppliers of these ingredients. Flour is perhaps the most competitive, but now just 30 companies operate the UK's 57 mills. The two largest companies account for approximately 40% of UK production with a further 20 companies producing significant quantities.

Threat of new entrants

Chances are, if you are thinking about starting up or growing in a market, there will be others doing the same too. If it is easy to enter your market, start-up costs are low and there are no barriers to entry such as IP protection, the threat could be high. Taking our baker as an example, he (or she) may be surprised to learn that there are nearly 10,000 other small bakeries operating around the UK. A thousand or so of those go out of business each year and around the same number start up. Other markets have quite different new entrant prospects. For example the 40,000 or so small hairdresser salons in the UK see many more new entrants than the bakery sector and the hotel and guest house business see far fewer.

Threat of substitutes

Can customers buy something else instead of your product or service? For example Apple, and to a lesser extent Sony, have laptop computers that are distinctive enough to make substitution difficult. Dell on the other hand faces intense competition from dozens of other suppliers with near identical products competing mostly on price alone. Customers can eat non-organic bread and perhaps save money, or they can bake it themselves at home.

Industry competition

The number and capability of competitors is one determinant of a business's relative power. Few competitors with relatively less attractive products or services lower the intensity of rivalry in a sector. For our baker the situation looks tough. The three main manufacturers (Warburton's, Allied Bakeries and Premier Foods) account for almost three-quarters of the bread market by value. In-store bakery (ISB) bread is bread that is baked in-store, and is now a feature of all major supermarkets and most large grocery stores. They can also be found in small grocers, butchers and other small shops, garage forecourts and restaurants. Then there are the 10,000 or so small independent bakeries, all fighting for a slice of the market.

Buyer power

In the food market, where our baker is situated, there are a few powerful supermarket buyers being supplied by tens of thousands of much smaller businesses. These are the classic conditions for buyers to exert power, usually dictating terms on price and payment terms. Even when a small business gets acceptable terms their dangers are not over. Giant companies can place big orders and so leave small businesses with a very narrow customer base.

Rivalry

These five forces of your research, which will help you plan strategy, are themselves influenced by external factors such as market growth rate: usually if a market is growing fast it is easier for a new business to get a foothold or expand into. If demand is contracting the reverse applies. It is always harder selling into a falling market, until conditions force out weaker players and supply and demand move back to near equilibrium.

> ### Startups Tip
> Avoid markets where there are a few big and powerful customers, hundreds of competitors and few suppliers. The best position for you to be is where the forces are weakest: thousands of small customers, plenty of sources of supply and no significant competitors.

Establishing your knowledge gaps

Working your way through the market knowledge checklist in Figure 2.2 will give you a good idea of where to concentrate your research efforts. Best to be totally honest here, and don't be afraid to fill up the right hand column with ideas for getting at the facts.

The rest of this chapter will arm you with the basic tools and resources to top up your knowledge base, and Chapters 3 and 4 will look in detail at getting to grips with customers and competitors.

Industry competition				Know the facts/plan for getting knowledge
Number of competitors	Lots	←→	Few	
Market share of top three companies	75%+	←→	25%-	
Easy market to get into	Very	←→	Hard	
Strong brand loyalty	Yes	←→	No	
Easy market to get out of	Yes	←→	No	
Competitors financially stronger	Yes	←→	No	
Buyer Power				
Number of potential customers	Lots	←→	Few	
Market share of top three customers	75%+	←→	25%-	
Price sensitivity	High	←→	No	
Buyer likely to move into your field	Yes	←→	No	
Threat of Substitutes				
Hard for customers to switch products	Yes	←→	No	
Cheaper alternatives on the market	Yes	←→	No	
Better quality products around	Yes	←→	No	
Better performing products out there	Yes	←→	No	
Threat of New Entrants				
Economies of scale make it hard	Yes	←→	No	
Capital intensive so tough to get going	Yes	←→	No	
Brand loyalty locks the market	Yes	←→	No	
Regulations make entry difficult	Yes	←→	No	
Access to marketing channels limited	Yes	←→	No	
Intellectual property restricts access	Yes	←→	No	
Supplier Power				
Market share of top three suppliers	75%+	←→	25%-	
Suppliers are bigger than their customers	Yes	←→	No	
We would be unimportant to suppliers	Yes	←→	No	
Suppliers could move easily into our field	Yes	←→	No	
Rivalry General Factors				
Our market is growing annually by	10%+	←→	-5%	
Technology is changing our industry	Fast	←→	Slow	
Generally, costs in your industry are rising	Fast	←→	Slow	
Profit margins in your industry are	Strong	←→	Weak	
There is a large untapped market to go at	Yes	←→	No	

Figure 2.2 Market knowledge checklist

The tools of the trade

Assuming you don't intend to commission professional market research, you will need to do the research yourself. This is no bad thing as it will let you see everything and not just the edited highlights that a research company is likely to provide. That's not to denigrate professionals, it's just that one of their key skills is to be concise. Unfortunately, markets are messy and sticking strictly to a scientific process only gets you so far. Business is perhaps more an art than a science.

But a more compelling reason for understanding how to use the tools is that market research should become an integral part in the ongoing life of your business. Competitors and customer needs change; products and services don't last forever. Once started, however, ongoing market research becomes easier, as you have existing customers (and staff) to question.

Fortunately, there are only two fundamental tools: desk research (where you are uncovering data that someone else has already gathered and made available in some form or other); and field research (where you or someone you employ has to create the information).

Libraries

One further free or nearly free tool at your disposal is libraries. There are thousands of libraries in the UK and tens of thousands elsewhere in the world, which between them contain more desk research data that any entrepreneur could ever ask for. As well as the fairly conventional lending services in the area of business books, these libraries also contain all the reference and research databases listed later in this chapter and many hundreds more. Libraries, in particular the reference libraries in larger towns and cities, also have internet access to their data, in various forms, and many offer fee-paying research services for business users, at fairly modest rates.

Apart from public libraries, there are hundreds of university libraries, specialist science and technology libraries and government collections of data, which can be accessed with little difficulty.

> ### Startups Tip
> Librarians are trained, among other things, to archive and retrieve information and data from their own libraries and increasingly from internet data sources. As such they represent an invaluable resource that entrepreneurs should tap into early in the research process.

Desk and field research methods

There is increasingly a great deal of secondary data available in published form, accessible either online or via business sections of public libraries throughout the UK, to enable business starters and growers both to quantify the size of market sectors they are entering and to determine trends in those markets. In addition to populations of cities and towns (helping to start quantification of markets), libraries frequently purchase Mintel Reports, involving studies of growth in different business sectors. Government statistics, showing trends in the economy, are also held (Annual Abstracts for the economy as a whole, Business Monitor for individual sectors).

If you plan to sell to companies or shops, Kompass and Kelly's directories list all company names and addresses (including buyers' telephone numbers). Many industrial sectors are represented by trade associations, which can provide information (see the Directory of British Associations, CBD Research), while chambers of commerce are good sources of reference for import/export markets.

The following list contains some readily available sources of desk research data you can use without incurring very much cost.

→ Chambers of commerce run import/export clubs and provide market research and online intelligence through a 150 country local network of chambers. Check out the International Chamber of Commerce World Business Organisation website (www.iccwbo.org).

→ Companies House (www.companieshouse.gov.uk) is the official repository of all company information in the UK. Its WebCHeck service offers a free of charge searchable company names and address index covering two million companies either by name or unique company registration number. You can use WebCHeck to purchase a company's latest accounts, giving details of sales, profits, margins, directors, shareholders and bank borrowings at a cost of £1 per company.

→ Doing Business (www.doingbusiness.org) is the World Bank's database that provides objective measures of business regulations across 183 countries and produces occasional reports on major cities within those countries. You can find out everything from the rules on opening and closing a business, trading across borders, tax rates, employment laws, enforcing contracts and much more. There is a tool for comparing countries to rank them by the criteria you consider most important.

→ FAME (Financial Analysis Made Easy) is a powerful database that contains information on 3.4 million companies in the UK and Ireland. The software lets you search for companies using your own criteria, combining as many conditions as you like. So, for example, you could identify competitors with the strongest and weakest financial position and so get an insight into how to compete with them. You can also identify those with the fastest and slowest rates of sales growth or best and worst profit margins, important facts to have to hand in any marketing armoury. FAME is available in business libraries and on CD from the publisher, which also offers a free trial.

→ Kelly's (www.kellysearch.co.uk) lists information on 200,000 product and service categories across 200 countries. Business contact details, basic product and service details and online catalogues are provided.

→ Kompass (www.kompass.com) claims to have details of 1.6 million UK companies, 23 million key product and service references, 3.2 million executive names, 744,000 trade and brand names and 50,000 Kompass classification codes in its UK directory. It also creates directory information in over 70 countries. Its website has a free access area that users may access without registration.

→ Thomas Global Register (www.thomasglobal.com) is an online directory in 11 languages with details of over 700,000 suppliers in 28 countries. It can be searched by industry sub-sector or name either for the world or by country.

→ Trade Association Forum (www.taforum.org) is the directory of trade associations on whose websites are links to industry-relevant online research sources. For example, you will find The Baby Products Association listed, at whose website you can find details of the 238 companies operating in that sector.

⇥ UK Trade & Investment (www.uktradeinvest.gov.uk) is the
    government agency that helps UK-based businesses succeed in
    "an increasingly global world". They provide information on doing
    business with every country and every business sector from
    aerospace to water.

Carrying out field research

This entails getting out and finding out essential facts that have not
been uncovered by desk research, either because the data hasn't been
collected, or because it is deficient in some important respect. Very
often you will find that while general market information is available,
say for our baker national information on organic bread, there is not
information for a particular town or region. Also, when the economic
climate changes, say from boom to bust, buying patterns may shift
quite suddenly, making desk research irrelevant.

The most common methods of carrying out field research are as
follows.

Observation

The power of observation as a method of gathering data lies in the
inconsistency between what people will say in an interview, or on
a questionnaire, and what they actually do. It's not that people are
necessarily lying, it's just that their capacity for self-deception is
often high. Customers may feel foolish admitting they have difficulty
understanding how to use a product or service and so would not
record that fact. That doesn't mean that they don't have a problem
and that a company would gain valuable information from finding out
about it.

So, observations can give valuable insights into how things look from
an outsider such as a customer, supplier or prospective employee. But
such insights will only be representative of the time the researcher was
observing and may not be indicative of the general level of service.
They are often used to provide contextual information alongside some
other research method.

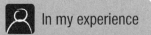
> ### In my experience
>
> ## Sophie Cornish and Holly Tucker, Notonthehighstreet.com
>
> "See enough people with a problem and you have a business opportunity. Working in the events and shopping sectors we realised there was a wealth of quirky and distinctive retailers without an affordable and effective method of selling their products. Most of these businesses did not have an online presence, and of the ones that did, there was virtually no e-commerce capability.
>
> "The businesses we spoke to were desperate for what we were offering: a way of reaching customers without lugging their products around the country attending really expensive trade fairs which could cost thousands to exhibit at."

Interviews

Talking and listening to people is the most basic and the most used method of conducting qualitative research. Interviews differ from surveys, for example in that they adhere less to a fixed set of questions but continually probe and cross-check information, building cumulatively on the knowledge gained from earlier answers. Nevertheless, interviewers at some point have to ask the questions that give them the specific data they need. Good interpersonal skills, sensitivity to the respondent, conducting the interviews at an appropriate time and place as well as having an appropriate sample are all vital to successful interviewing.

Focus groups

Focus groups are a form of multiple interview with small groups of around eight to 10 people selected with certain key attributes in mind, specific knowledge, experience or socio-economic characteristics for example. Participants are invited to attend informal discussion sessions of no more than two hours' duration on a particular topic. You have probably already carried out or participated in one but without calling it a focus group.

Focus groups need careful managing to make sure you don't end up with bland generalities. Apple, for example, is particularly critical of the process. Henry Ford summed up this position aptly in this attributed quote: "If I'd have asked my customers what they wanted, they would have told me 'a faster horse'."

For more basic research decisions on product design, pricing and packaging, for example, focus groups are used extensively by most of the major consumer brands. The advantages of using a focus group over interviews include efficiency, as you can get 10 opinions in around twice the time it takes to conduct an interview; and by listening to other people's comments often more ideas, opinions and experiences and insights can be gained. It is also easier to take notes of the discussion, as this is expected and less threatening in a group situation. But as with interviews, focus groups rely on the views of a small sample and so are not truly representative of any body of opinion.

In my experience

Simon Woodroffe, YO! Sushi

"I was having lunch with a Japanese man who said, 'What you should do Simon is a conveyor belt sushi bar with girls in black PVC mini-skirts.' I found out there were 3,000 of them in Japan."

Surveys

The most common field research method is the survey. This is a near-ubiquitous tool used by organisations to get a handle on almost everything from measuring market potential and assessing customer satisfaction to getting the views on almost any issue surrounding a product or service.

Around half of all surveys are conducted face to face, considered best for tackling consumer markets. Next in popularity come telephone, email and web surveys, which work well with companies and organisations. Postal surveys, once very popular, now account for less than 10% of survey work.

Telephone interviewing requires a very positive attitude, courtesy, an ability not to talk too quickly and to listen while sticking to a rigid questionnaire. Low response rates on postal services (less than 10% is normal) can be improved by accompanying letters explaining the questionnaire's purpose and why respondents should reply, by offering rewards for completed questionnaires (a small gift), by sending reminder letters and, of course, by providing pre-paid reply envelopes. Personally addressed email questionnaires have secured higher response rates – as high as 10%–15% – as recipients have a greater tendency to read and respond to email received in their private email boxes. However, unsolicited emails ('spam') will mostly be ignored: the key to success is the same as with postal surveys – the mailing should feature an explanatory letter and incentives for the recipient to 'open' the questionnaire.

In my experience

Edwina Dunn and Clive Humby, dunnhumby

"We decided to carry out a survey called 'Computers in Marketing', looking at the role of computers in marketing and analysing data. We approached 1,000 companies and received 110 responses. The survey gained us extensive press coverage in the trade press, enabling us to build our business profile and achieve positive PR."

Complaints

Founder of foreign exchange business Currencies Direct, Mayank Patel, sees customer complaints as a valuable learning opportunity: "Treat a customer complaint with absolute seriousness. Think of it as an asset, because someone is telling you free of charge what could be better in your business. Somebody could tell you how to turn something around and make your proposition better. Don't throw that in the bin thinking 'Oh, we've got a customer that's complaining or a whinging customer.' A management consultant will charge you tens of thousands of pounds for what that customer is telling you for nothing."

Questionnaire design

1. Keep the number of questions to a minimum.
2. Keep the questions simple! Answers should be either 'Yes/No/Don't know' or offer at least four alternatives.
3. Avoid ambiguity – make sure the respondent really understands the question (avoid 'generally', 'usually', 'regularly').
4. Look for factual answers; avoid opinions.
5. Make sure at the beginning you have a cut-out question to eliminate unsuitable respondents (eg those who never use the product/service).
6. At the end, make sure you have an identifying question to show the cross-section of respondents.

Construct the research sample population

Just asking questions of anyone you come across is unlikely to give you reliable information. Unless you put some basic statistical method into your research you will be largely wasting time and money. You may also find that anyone reading your business plan or listening to your presentation will be underwhelmed if you can't explain how you went about gathering your data.

It isn't usually possible or even desirable to include every possible customer or competitor in your research. Instead you would select a sample of people, who represent the whole population being surveyed. Sampling saves time and money and can be more accurate than surveying an entire population. If your market is pet owners, talking to all of them, even in a small geographical area, may take months. By the time you have completed your survey the first people questioned may have changed their opinion, or the whole environment may have altered in some material way.

There are two main methods of sampling which can help ensure you have a population that will provide reliable data.

Probability sampling

This is done to statistical rules with each member of the sample population having a known chance of being selected. A selection is made from the whole of a population using a method that ensures randomness. This could be achieved by picking names out of a hat or by using random number tables. You can find a random number generator and a more detailed explanation of the subject at www.stattrek.com/Tables/Random.aspx.

Non-probability sampling

This is used when probability sampling is not possible, for example when no list of the population exists or when the population is not stable over time, for example an airport booking hall. This type of sampling includes such methods as calling for volunteers or on-the-street interviews and using students as guinea pigs in an experiment.

This method can be further refined by selecting people or groups of people that you believe will result in a group that is representative of the population as a whole. Further refinement can be applied to ensure the people sampled represent the overall population in some important respect. For example, if we know that 60% of pet owners are women, then we might construct our sample with that proportion of women in it.

> ### Startups Tip
> If time is short (and money isn't), consider using the services of a professional market research company. As a rough guide to costs, a business-to-business survey comprising 200 interviews with executives responsible for office equipment purchasing decisions cost one company £12,000. Twenty in-depth interviews with consumers who are regular users of certain banking services cost £8,000.

Using the internet

The internet is a rich source of market data, much of it free and immediately available. But you can't always be certain that the information is reliable or free of bias as it can be difficult (if not impossible) to always work out who exactly is providing it. That being said, you can get some valuable pointers as to whether what you plan to sell has a market, how big that market is and who else trades in that space. The following sources should be your starting point.

⇨ Google Trends (www.google.co.uk/trends) provides a snapshot on what the world is most interested in at any one moment. For example, if you are thinking of starting a business selling clothes for kids, entering that into the search pane would produce a snazzy graph showing how interest measured by the number of searches is growing (or contracting) since January 2004 (when Google started collecting the data). You could also perhaps see that Dublin has the greatest interest, closely followed by Poplar, in London. You could tweak the graph to show seasonality thus showing that 'demand' peaks (for example) in November and bottoms out in January – the 'Christmas effect'.

⇨ Google News (www.google.com), which you can tap into by selecting 'News' on the horizontal menu at the top of the page under the Google banner. Here you will find links to any newspaper article anywhere in the world covering a particular topic. Asking for information on baby clothes will reveal recent articles on how much the average family spends on baby clothes, the launch of a thrift store specialising in second-hand baby clothes and the launch of an organic baby clothes catalogue.

⇨ Microsoft (www.adlab.microsoft.com/Audience-Intelligence.aspx) is testing a product that can give you a mass of data on market demographics (age, sex, income, etc), purchase intentions and a search funnel tool that helps you understand how your market searches the internet. Using the demographics tool you could, for example, find that 76% of people showing an interest in baby clothes are female (and surprisingly 24% are male). You could also find that the peak age group is the 25–34-year-olds and the lowest is the under 18s, followed by the over 50s.

⇢ Blogs are sites where people, informed and ignorant, converse about a particular topic. The information on blogs is more straw in the wind than fact. Globe of Blogs (www.globeofblogs.com) claims to be the first comprehensive world weblog directory. Google (www.blogsearch.google.com) is also a search engine to the world's blogs.

⇢ Trade Association Forum (www.taforum.org) is the directory of trade associations on whose websites are links to industry relevant online research sources. For example, you will find The Baby Products Association listed, at whose website you can find details of the companies operating in that sector.

Doing surveys online

If you have email addresses for the sample you want to survey, or have a website with a reasonable amount of traffic, there are a couple of big advantages to carrying out your survey online. In the first place it will be quicker and probably cheaper than any other method. However, the most compelling reason is that collecting data this way makes it easy to analyse as you don't have to transcribe it to a spreadsheet.

> **Startups Tip**
> Check out companies such as Free Online Surveys (www.free-online-surveys.co.uk) and Zoomerang (www.zoomerang.com/web/signup/Basic.aspx), which provide software that lets you carry out online surveys and analyse the data quickly. Most of these organisations offer free trials.

Testing the market

The ultimate form of market research is to find some real customers to buy and use your product or service before you spend too much time and money in setting up. The ideal way to do this is to sell into a limited area or small section of your market. In that way, if things don't quite work out as you expect you won't have upset too many people.

This may involve buying in a small quantity of product as you need to fulfil the order in order to fully test your ideas. Once you have found a small number of people who are happy with your product, price, delivery/execution, and have paid up, then you can proceed with a bit more confidence than if all your ideas are just on paper.

Pick potential customers whose demand is likely to be small and easy to meet. For example, if you are going to run a bookkeeping business select five to 10 small businesses from an area reasonably close to home and make your pitch. The same approach would work with gardening, baby sitting or any other service-related venture. It's a little more difficult with products, but you could buy a small quantity of similar items in from a competitor or make up a trial batch yourself.

> ### In my experience
>
>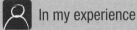
>
> ### Nick Jenkins, Moonpig
>
> "During my last weeks at Cranfield I took my idea to Paperlink, a successful greeting card publishing company without an online presence, and offered them a small stake in the company if they would let the as-yet-unnamed company use their greetings cards. Miraculously, they agreed, and this was enough to convince me I had an idea worth pursuing."

Understanding the data

The most common way statistics are considered is around a single figure that claims in some way to be representative of a population at large. This is usually referred to as an average. There are three principal ways of measuring an average, and these are the most often confused and frequently misrepresented set of numbers in any business plan!

> ### Startups Tip
> Showing which type of 'average' you are using when presenting research information in your business plan will add greatly to your credibility.

To analyse any information gathered from market research you first need a 'dataset' such as that in Table 2.1.

TABLE 2.1: Competitor selling prices

Competitor	Selling price (£)
1	30
2	40
3	10
4	15
5	10

The mean (or average)

This is the most common measure to express information and is used as a rough and ready check for many types of data. In the example above, adding up the prices (£105) and dividing by the number of competitors (5) you arrive at a mean, or average, selling price of £21.

The median

The median is the value at the mid-point of a dataset. Recasting the figures in Table 2.1 puts company 4's selling price of £15 in that position, with two higher and two lower prices. You can find out more about medians and when to use them on the Purplemath website (www. purplemath.com/modules/meanmode.htm).

The mode

The mode is the most frequently occurring observation in a dataset; in this example the mode is £10. So, if we were surveying a sample of customers across the whole market we would expect more of them to say they were paying £10 for their products, though (as we know) the average price is £21.

Range

As well as measuring how values cluster around a central value, to make full use of the dataset we need to establish how much those values could vary. The range helps here and is calculated as the maximum figure minus the minimum figure. In the example being used here, the range is £40 − £10 = £30. This figure gives us an idea of how dispersed the data are and so how meaningful say the average figure alone might be.

Checklist

☑ **Formulate the problem**: before embarking on your market research you should first set clear and precise objectives, rather than just setting out to find interesting general information about the market.

☑ **Decide the budget**: market research will not be free even if you do it yourself. At the very least there will be your time. Whatever the cost of research, you need to assess its value to you when you are setting your budget. If getting it wrong would cost £100,000, £5,000 spent on market research might be a good investment.

☑ **Process and analyse the data**: the raw market research data needs to be analysed and turned into information to guide the decisions that go into your business plan.

☑ **Select the research technique**: if you cannot find the data you require from desk research, you will need to go out and find the data yourself.

🖝 *CHAPTER 3*

Understanding your market: customers

📖 What's in this chapter?

Businesses can survive without many things, but customers are not one of them. Customers don't just show up when a business gets off the ground: they are out there already and, for the most part, surviving pretty well without you. Your product, however innovative or new, is for the most part only going to displace, dislodge or dislocate an existing supplier's offering much as emails displaced telegrams, and they in turn overtook the network of pony express-type courier services operating around the globe.

From the outset your business plan has to be based on a sound appreciation of exactly what your product or service can deliver in terms of value to its potential user base.

In this chapter we'll cover:

→ *products and services: defining their relationship*

Products and services: defining their relationship

Marketing experts define a product as having a "bundle of needs-satisfying attributes". A 'product' can have a tangible, physical element as well as an intangible yet vital ingredient. Just think how satisfied you would be getting a great meal, made from the best ingredients, served by a rude, casual waiter delivered two hours after you placed your order.

The amount of value to the customer, and potential revenue to the supplier, varies from the almost entirely tangible, for example a staple 'commodity' such as milk, to a virtual intangible medical consultation (see Figure 3.1). Some product or service elements can even be found at either end of the product–service continuum. Milk may be differentiated by better branding, and you will probably end up with a written report on your medical condition.

The founder of a successful cosmetics firm, when asked what he did, replied: "In the factories we make perfume, in the shops we sell

Figure 3.1 The product–service continuum

dreams." Positioning your business proposition calls for an equally sound and succinct grasp of what your customers really are after.

Why customers buy: Maslow's hierarchy of needs

Those of us in business usually start out defining our business in physical terms. Customers, on the other hand, see businesses having as their primary value the ability to satisfy their needs. Even firms that adopt customer satisfaction, or even delight, as their stated maxim often find it a more complex goal than it first appears.

Take the customers of a designer clothing company, by way of an example. They make clothes sure enough: but the primary customer need they are aiming to satisfy is not either to preserve their customer's modesty or to keep them warm. The need they are aiming for is very different: their goal is to ensure their customers feel fashionably dressed, which is about the way people interact with each other and how they feel about themselves; just splashing say a tog rating showing the thermal properties of the fabric, as you would say a duvet, would cut no ice with this business's clients.

Until you have clearly defined the needs of your customers you cannot begin to assemble a product or service to satisfy them. Fortunately, help is at hand. An American psychologist Abraham Maslow, who taught at Brandeis University, Boston, a top US business school, demonstrated in his research that "all customers are goal seekers who gratify their needs by purchase and consumption". He then went a bit further and classified consumer needs into a five-stage pyramid he called the 'hierarchy of needs' (see Figure 3.2 on the opposite page).

Self-actualisation

This is the summit of Maslow's hierarchy in which people are looking for truth, wisdom, justice and purpose. It's a need that is never fully satisfied and, according to Maslow, only a very small percentage of people ever reach the point where they are prepared to pay much

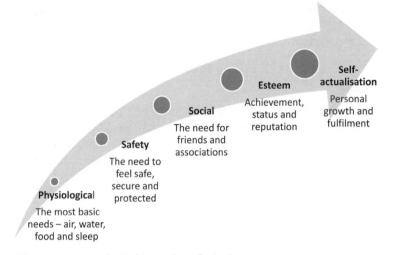

Figure 3.2 Maslow's hierarchy of needs

money to satisfy such needs. It is left to the likes of Bill Gates and Warren Buffett to give away billions to form foundations to dispose their wealth on worthy causes. The rest of us scrabble around further down the hierarchy.

Esteem

Here people are concerned with such matters as self-respect, achievement, attention, recognition and reputation. The benefits customers are looking for include the feeling that others will think better of them if they have a particular product. Much of brand marketing is aimed at making consumers believe that conspicuously wearing the maker's label or logo will earn them 'respect'. Understanding how this part of Maslow's hierarchy works was vital to the founders of Responsibletravel.com (www.responsibletravel. com), founded eight years ago with backing from the late Dame Anita Roddick (Body Shop) in Justin Francis's front room in Brighton, with his partner Harold Goodwin. Setting out to be the world's first company to offer environmentally responsible travel and holidays, they were one of the first companies to offer carbon offset schemes for travellers. They boast that they turn away more tour companies trying to list on their site than they accept. The site appeals to consumers who want to be recognised in their communities as being socially responsible.

Social

The need for friends, belonging to associations, clubs or other groups, and the need to give and get love are all social needs. After 'lower' needs have been met these needs that relate to interacting with other people come to the fore. Hotel Chocolat (www.hotelchocolat.co.uk), founded by Angus Thirlwell and Peter Harris in their kitchen, is a good example of a business based on meeting social needs. They market home-delivered luxury chocolates but generate sales by conducting tasting clubs to check out products each month. The concept of the club is that you invite friends round and, using the firm's scoring system, rate and give feedback on the chocolates.

Safety

The second most basic need of consumers is to feel safe and secure. People who feel they are in harm's way, either through their general environment or because of the product or service on offer, will not be over-interested in having their higher needs met. When Charles Rigby set up World Challenge (www.world-challenge.co.uk) to market challenging expeditions to exotic locations around the world, with the aim of taking young people up to around 19 years of age out of their comfort zones and teaching them how to overcome adversity, he knew he had a challenge of his own on his hands: how to make an activity simultaneously exciting and apparently dangerous to teenagers, while being safe enough for the parents writing the cheques to feel comfortable. Six full sections on the World Challenge website are devoted to explaining the safety measures the company takes to ensure that unacceptable risks are eliminated as far as is humanly possible.

Physiological

Air, water, sleep and food are all absolutely essential to sustain life. Until these basic needs are satisfied, higher needs such as self-esteem will not be considered.

What customers buy: features, benefits, proofs

While understanding customer needs is vital, it is not sufficient on its own to help put together a saleable proposition. Before you can do that you have to understand the specific benefits customers will get when they purchase your product.

> ## JARGON BUSTER
>
> Features are what a product or service has or is, and benefits are what the product does for the customer.

When Nigel Apperley founded his business, Internet Cameras Direct, now Internet Direct (www.internetdirect.co.uk) and part of the AIM listed eXpansys plc, while a student at business school, he knew there was no point in telling customers about SLRs (single lens reflexes) or shutter speeds. These are not the end products that customers want: they are looking at the convenience and economy of buying direct. He planned to follow the Dell Computer direct sales model. Within three years Apperley had an annual turnover in excess of £20 million and had moved a long way from his home-based beginnings.

TABLE 3.1: Example of product features, benefits and proofs

Features	Benefits	Proofs
Our maternity clothes are designed by fashion experts	You get to look and feel great.	See the press comments in fashion magazines
Our bookkeeping system is approved by HM Revenue and Customs	You can sleep at night	Our system is rated No 1 by the Accounting Evaluation Centre
Our airline has the best punctuality record	You can make your travel plans with reasonable certainty	Statistics published by International Association of Travel Agents

Table 3.1 provides examples of product features and benefits, which has been extended to include proofs showing how the benefits will be delivered. The essential element to remember here is that the customer only wants to pay for benefits, while the seller has to pick up the tab for all the features, whether or not the customers sees them as valuable. Benefits will provide the 'copy' for a business's advertising and promotional activities.

In my experience

Nick Jenkins, Moonpig

"Customers are not interested in the technology, they are interested in the reaction the card gets when the recipient opens it."

B2B buyer criteria

There is a popular theory that business buyers are hard-nosed, cold-hearted Scrooges, making entirely rational choices with the sole goal of doing the best they can for their shareholders. If this were really the case an awful lot of promotional gift suppliers would be out of business. Pharmaceutical companies could fire their sales forces, slashing costs by billions. All doctors and pharmacists would have to do is read the research on drugs and prescribe accordingly. That probably wouldn't take any more time than listening to a rep make their pitch.

At the end of the day people buy from people, and that's where Maslow's needs swing back into play. "No one ever got fired buying IBM" was a much quoted phrase in buying departments in the days when IBM's main business was selling computers. This simply meant that the buyer could feel secure making that decision as IBM's reputation was high. Buying anywhere else, even if the specification was better and the price lower, was personally risky. IBM's sales force could use the buyer's need to feel safe to great advantage in their presentations.

When understanding the needs of business buyers, it is important to keep in mind that there are at least three major categories of people who have a role to play in the B2B buying decision, and whose needs have to be considered in any analysis of a business market.

The user, or end customer

This is the recipient of any final benefits associated with the product or service, much as with an individual consumer. Functionality will be vital for this group.

The specifier

Though specifiers may not use (or even see) their purchases, they will want to be sure the end user's needs are met in terms of performance, delivery and any other important parameters. Their 'customer' is both the end user and the budget holder of the cost centre concerned. There may even be conflict between the two (or more) 'customer' groups. For example, in the case of, say, hotel toiletries, those responsible for marketing the rooms will want high-quality product to enhance their offer while the hotel manager will have cost concerns, and the people responsible for actually putting the product in place will be interested only in any handling and packaging issues.

The non-consuming buyer

This is the person who actually places the order. They will be basing their decision on a specification drawn up by someone else, but they will also have individual needs. Some of their needs are similar to those of a specifier, except they will have price at or near the top of their needs.

Sizing up the relevant market

The size of the market you intend to get into is a key figure that will be used by anyone reading your business plan, yourself included. That figure represents the total scope of the opportunity ahead and is the starting point in shaping your marketing strategy. Now, in principle, this is not too difficult. Desk research (see Chapter 2) will yield a sizeable harvest of statistics of varying degrees of reliability. If bread is your business you will be able to discover rapidly that the consumption of bread in Europe is £10 billion a year. But bread is a very broad industry.

The industry-wide definition of bread includes sliced and unsliced bread, rolls, bakery snacks and speciality breads. It covers plant-baked products, those that are baked by in-store bakers, and products sold through craft bakers.

Assessing the relevant market, then, involves refining global statistics to provide the real scope of your market. If your business only operates in the UK the market is worth over £2.7 billion, equivalent to 12 million loaves a day, one of the largest sectors in food. If you are only operating in the craft bakery segment, the relevant market shrinks down to £13.5 million; this in turn contracts still further to £9.7 million if you are, say, only operating within the M25.

This is the hurdle that nine out of every 10 business plans fails to cross. Entrepreneurs like to think big, but a business plan based on attacking the £10 billion European bread market, rather than the much smaller near-£10 million market for craft bread products they are really going into, will lack all credibility.

Segmenting the market

Customers have different needs with different levels of intensity. Everyone has safety in mind, but you will be more concerned about that when you chose an airline than when you buy a pen. That in turn means that you need to organise your marketing effort so as to address those individual needs; however, trying to satisfy everyone may mean that you end up satisfying no one fully.

The marketing process that helps us deal with this seemingly impossible task is market segmentation.

JARGON BUSTER

Market segmentation describes the process of categorising customers into groups by factors such as age, education or income and then tailoring aspects of your offer so as to appeal to them in particular.

Worthwhile criteria

Not all market segments are equally attractive, or perhaps even worth tackling. These are four useful rules to help decide if a market segment is worth building into your business plan.

1. **Measurability.** Can you estimate how many customers are in the segment? Are there enough to make it worth offering something 'different'?
2. **Accessibility.** Can you communicate with these customers, preferably in a way that reaches them on an individual basis? For example, you could reach the over-50s by advertising in a specialist 'older people's' magazine with reasonable confidence that younger people will not read it. So, if you were trying to promote Scrabble with tiles 50% larger, you might prefer that young people did not hear about it. If they did, it might give the product an old-fashioned image.
3. **Open to profitable development.** The customers must have money to spend on the benefits that you propose to offer. One of the fastest growing market segments comprises occupants of retirement homes, but there is not much evidence that they have the cash to spend on new products and services, however worthwhile or desirable.
4. **Size.** A segment has to be large enough to be worth your exploiting it, but perhaps not so large as to attract larger competitors.

Segmentation is an important marketing process, as it helps to bring customers more sharply into focus, classifies them into manageable groups, and allows you to focus on one or more niches. It has wide-ranging implications for other marketing decisions. For example, the same product can be priced differently according to the intensity of customers' needs. The first- and second-class post is one example, off-peak rail travel another. It is also a continuous process that needs to be carried out periodically, for example when strategies are being reviewed.

> **In my experience**
>
> ## Sophie Cornish, Notonthehighstreet.com
>
> "Catering for non-web savvy sellers and customers is fundamental to our whole concept, so every aspect of the site has been designed accordingly, with detailed user guides and a dedicated support team on call to walk clients through it all."

Methods of segmentation

There are several ways by which markets can be segmented.

Psychographic

This approach divides individual consumers into social groups such as 'Yuckies' (young, unwitting, costly kids – who are still at home at 30), 'Yuppies' (young, upwardly mobile professionals), 'Bumps' (borrowed-to-the-hilt, upwardly mobile, professional show-offs) and 'Jollies' (jet-setting oldies with lots of loot).

These categories try to show how social behaviour influences buyer behaviour. Forrester Research, an internet research house, claims that when it comes to determining whether consumers will or will not go on the internet, how much they'll spend and what they'll buy, demographic factors such as age, race and gender don't matter anywhere near as much as the consumers' attitudes towards technology. Forrester uses this concept, together with its research, to produce Technographics® market segments as an aid to understanding people's behaviour as digital consumers. Forrester has used two categories – technology optimists and technology pessimists – alongside income and what it calls 'primary motivation' (career, family and entertainment) to divide the whole market. Each segment is given a new name: 'Techno-strivers', 'Digital Hopefuls' and so forth.

Benefit segmentation

This process recognises that different people can get different satisfaction from the same product or service. The classic marketing story used to explain this is that of toothpaste companies which target those motivated largely by health emphasising clinical benefits, while whiteness as cosmetic appeal is pitched at another group. Lastminute. com claims two quite distinctive benefits for its users. First, it aims to offer people bargains that appeal because of price and value. Second, it offers the benefit of immediacy. This idea is rather akin to the impulse-buy products placed at checkout tills, which you never thought of buying until you bumped into them on your way out. Whether 10 days on a beach in Goa or a trip to Istanbul are the types of things people 'pop in their baskets' before turning off their computers is another question.

Geographical

This form of segmentation arises when different locations have different needs. For example, an inner-city location may be a heavy user of motorcycle dispatch services, but a light user of gardening products.

Industrial

This groups together commercial customers according to a combination of their geographical location, principal business activity, relative size, frequency of product use, buying policies and a range of other factors. Logical Holdings is an e-business solutions and service company that floated for over £1 billion on the London Stock Exchange and TechMark index, making it one of the UK's biggest information technology (IT) companies. It was formed from about 30 acquisitions of small(ish) businesses. The company was founded by Rikke Helms, formerly head of IBM's E-Commerce Solutions portfolio. Her company split the market into three segments – small, medium-sized and big – tailoring its services specifically for each.

Multivariant

This segments markets using more than one variable. It can give a more precise picture of a market than using just one factor.

Specifiers, users and customers

When analysing market segments you should also keep in mind that there are at least three major categories of people who have a role to play in the buying decision, and so whose needs have to be considered in any analysis of a market.

⇝ The user, or end customer, will be the recipient of any final benefits associated with the product.

⇝ The specifier will want to be sure the end users needs are met in terms of performance, delivery and any other important parameters. Their 'customer' is both the end user and the budget holder of the cost centre concerned.

⇝ The non-consuming buyer, who places the order, also has individual needs. Some of their needs are similar to those of a specifier, except they will have price at or near the top of their needs. A particular category here is those buying gifts. Once again, their needs and those of the recipient may be dissimilar. For example, those buying gifts are as concerned with packaging as with content. Watches, pens, perfumes and fine wines are all gifts whose packaging is paramount at the point of purchase. Yet for the user they are often things to be immediately discarded.

Knowing who will buy first

However carefully your market is segmented, not every customer within a segment has an equal desire or need for your services. Word spreads slowly as the message is diffused throughout the various customer groups. Even then it is noticeable that generally it is the more adventurous types who buy at first. Only after these 'innovators' have given their seal of approval do the 'followers' come along. Research shows that this adoption process, as it is known, moves through five distinct customer characteristics, from Innovators to Laggards, with the overall population being different for each group (see Figure 3.3).

Let's suppose our hypothetical organic baker has identified a key market segment of affluent professionals within five miles of his

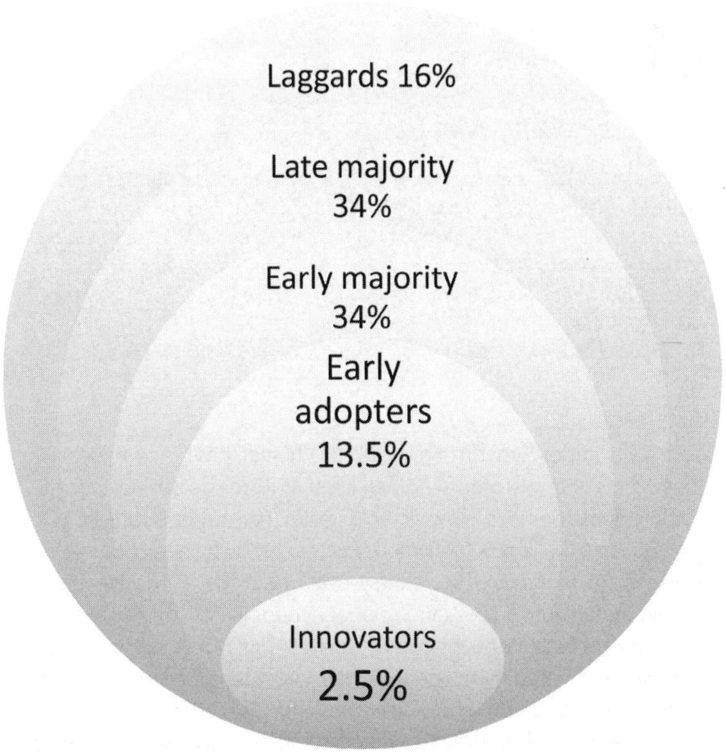

Laggards 16%

Late majority
34%

Early majority
34%

Early
adopters
13.5%

Innovators
2.5%

Figure 3.3 The product/service adoption process

bakery. Desk research shows that there are 100,000 people who meet the profile of an ideal customer, but then the initial market open for exploitation at the outset may be as low as 2,500, which is the 2.5% of innovators.

This adoption process, from the 2.5% of innovators who make up a new business's first customers, through to the Laggards, is most noticeable with truly innovative and relatively costly goods and services, but the general trend is true for all businesses. Until you have sold to the innovators, significant sales cannot be achieved. So, an important first task is to identify your market's innovators and tailor your initial proposition accordingly.

> ### In my experience
>
> ## Nick Jenkins, Moonpig
>
> The real growth of the Moonpig has been viral, spreading out from the more adventurous card buyers to the whole market. Nick remarks: "If it were as simple as spending lots of money on TV then everybody would be doing it. What's really made it work is customers spreading word about the product themselves. If you buy a card and take it to a party it gets passed around."

Founder of Charles Tyrwhitt Shirts, Nick Wheeler, has his own ideas on finding his first customers: "When I first started the business, one of the big questions was 'How do you start a mail-order business?' when you don't have any customers. I was very young and prepared to do anything and everything all day, every hour that God gave me. And I remember, just after Alan Sugar launched his Amstrad computer and made a fortune, I bought one of them. It was word processing for the masses and I used to sit there day and night tapping in names and addresses. I had a cousin who was in the 17th/21st Lancers and he gave me the address book of the old officers there and I just tapped them all in. And then I printed them all out and signed every letter. There were just thousands of letters, because I wanted it to be personal. I've always hated that idea that there's just so much direct mail around and it's just so boring and looks like it's just come out of a computer, and although mine was out of a computer it was personally signed, with my ink. I did everything and I think that made it different. And I think that's what got people going and people recognised that and started to buy the shirts."

Checklist

✓ Describe the main characteristics of your potential customers.

✓ Divide those customers into separate market segments and identify the main characteristics of each segment.

✓ Identify the needs that your product or service will satisfy for each key market segment.

✓ Match the features of your product/service to the benefits on offer to customers in each of your chosen market segments. Provide proof where possible.

✓ Identify the innovators in each of your key market segments.

↩ *CHAPTER 4*

Understanding your market: competitors

📖 What's in this chapter?

Researching the competition is often a time consuming and frustrating job, but there are important lessons to be learnt from their successes and failures. Some of the information that would be of most value to you will not be available. For example, it is particularly difficult to find information relating to size and profitability of small businesses, as they don't have to reveal much in their audited accounts. In fact, many don't even have to have their accounts audited. For these and for many aspects of competitor analysis you may have to make educated guesses that can be refined at a later date.

In this chapter we'll cover:

⟶ assessing your direct competitors

⟶ using 'SWOT analysis': strengths, weaknesses, opportunities and threats

→ Perceptual Mapping: a way to access your relative value proposition

→ reviewing substitutes

→ figuring out how the competition will react

→ estimating what new players could enter the market.

Assessing your direct competitors

When you begin your research, start by listing your key competitors. If necessary, classify them further into 'primary', 'secondary', 'potential' etc.

There are two reasons for doing this. First, you need to limit the number of businesses that you will do your research on to a workable number. If you try to research 25 businesses in depth, you won't have time to do anything else. If you end up with more than 10 or 12 primary competitors, you should probably think very carefully about whether or not this is a good market to get into, as the level of rivalry may make it hard to make a profit. Anyone reading your business plan would need convincing on that score. Second, you may want to classify competitors into primary and secondary since your marketing strategy may be different for each group.

Below are some of the issues your competitor research should set out to discover, recognising that some areas may be less relevant to certain types of businesses. You will find detailed explanations of these areas in the chapters that follow.

Find out your competitors':

- product range
- selling prices
- sales turnover, profit, profit margin, stock levels
- financial strength – retained profits, borrowings, shareholder base
- quality of product and/or service
- hours of operation
- number and ability of staff
- management structure
- servicing, warranties and packaging
- methods of selling: distribution channels
- credit terms: volume discounts
- location: advertising and promotion
- reputation of and/or principals
- length of time in business
- advertising strategy
- website proposition – position on Google etc.

> ### Startups Tip
> You may be able to get some valuable information from the
> annual accounts that each company has to file at Companies House.
> However, you should be aware that these are often not filed when
> required, or they may be incomplete, or contain information of no
> value. Further sources of information are local business directories such
> as Kelly's.
>
> In fact, the easiest way to find out what your competitors are doing right
> or wrong is to try them out. Even if you don't actually buy or even need
> what they sell there is nothing in the rules that says you can't enquire.

Using 'SWOT analysis': strengths, weaknesses, opportunities and threats

SWOT is a general purpose tool that was developed in the late 1960s
and consists of a cross with space in each quadrant to summarise your
findings (see Figure 4.1). Two important and often ignored factors to
take into account when carrying out a SWOT analysis are given below.

→ It is most effective when applied to individual market
segments, as a strength in one segment could be a weakness in
another. For example, stressing the low alcohol content of a
drink may enhance its appeal, say, to responsible adults while
reducing the brand's attraction to younger consumers.

→ You need to focus on your position relative to your
competitors. If you and all your competitors have got new
facilities, a sound team, access to cash and spare capacity then
these, though valuable, are not relative strengths. Similarly, if
there is a national shortage of trained technicians in your
sector, and they are a vital component of your business,
although not exactly good news, it is not a relative weakness.

In the example in Figure 4.1, the SWOT analysis is restricted to a
handful of areas, although in practice the list might run to a dozen
or more areas within each of the four quadrants. The purpose of the

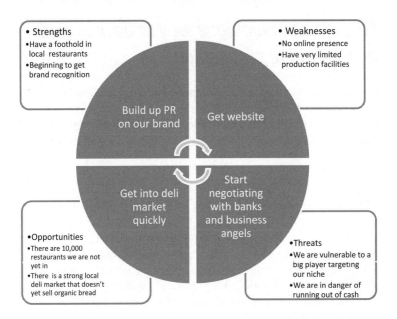

Figure 4.1 Example SWOT chart for a new organic baker

SWOT analysis is to suggest possible ways to improve the competitive position while minimising the dangers of perceived threats. This SWOT would suggest that to have a realistic chance of success, the business plan should show what additional production facilities are required and what cash is required. It should also outline plans to launch a website and get a presence in the deli sector.

SWOT is a useful method of pulling together a large amount of information on your competitors in a way that is easy to assimilate.

Perceptual Mapping: a way to access your relative value proposition

Perceptual or positioning maps are a useful marketing tool used to position products and services relative to competitors on two dimensions. In Figure 4.2, the position of companies competing in the bread market are compared on price and quality, on a spectrum from low to high.

Similar maps can be produced for any combination of variables that are of importance to customers – availability, product range, after-sales support, market image and so on. The technique is used in a variety of ways, including highlighting possible market gaps when one quadrant is devoid of players, suggesting areas to be built on or extended. In the example in Figure 4.2, there is a scope for our organic baker to move up a level in price. It can also be used in conjunction with your SWOT analysis to identify areas in which to create a competitive edge.

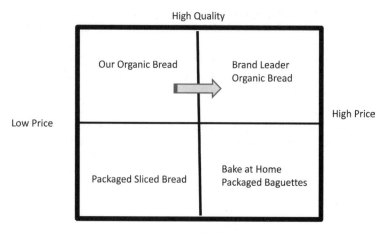

Figure 4.2 Perceptual Mapping

Reviewing substitutes

There is no easy way to identify what substitutes will come along, or when they might arrive. But the old adage "if something looks too good to be true, then it probably is" applies here. Things to look out for include the following.

⇨ Substitutes: if there are unsustainable pressures on your customers' costs then expect them to start looking for alternatives and for nimble competitors to enter the market. Ultimately, the main barrier to customers moving across to a substitute is the cost of switching.

⇨ Close substitutes: Coca-Cola faces direct competition from Pepsi, but has Fanta, juices, tea, coffee, milk, chocolate drinks, bottled water and any other product that provide customers with the same benefit – having their thirst quenched.

⇨ Partial substitutes: cinema, theatres, television, pay television, film hire and sales of DVDs all occupying roughly the same space in the entertainment market. Each of these products will have some loyal customers and some who move seamlessly between two or more of them. The threat may be weak, but it is nevertheless real.

⇨ Alternatives: these are products that are nearly below the radar. A classic example is the array of convenience products placed near the end of a supermarket checkout till. The link between chocolate, chewing gum, a torch, a cut-price video and a disposable barbecue is not obvious. However, these all compete for the same discretionary spending power, so buying one of these products can mean that another won't be bought.

> ## Brainstorming
>
> Brainstorming is a useful technique to use when considering what else your customers could spend their money on that would meet some or all of their needs. Get together with people whose opinions you value; put up as many ideas on the subject as you can generate, using a flipchart; don't allow any discussion until you have exhausted the ideas; then eliminate the totally impossible options. Those ideas left may constitute substitutes to your product or service.

Figuring out how the competition will react

Helmuth von Moltke, chief of staff of the Prussian Army for 30 years and regarded as one of the great strategists, memorably said, "No battle plan survives contact with the enemy." With this in mind it follows that no business plan should be written that doesn't take into account an appreciation of how the competition is likely to react once your product or service hits the market.

There are three possible competitor reactions to a new entrant to a market.

1. **No response:** this is the most common reaction if your entry poses no significant threat to existing suppliers. This is almost invariably the case where competitors are significantly bigger and well entrenched. Yahoo, to its cost, initially ignored Google's entry into the market, seeing the business as an underfunded upstart.

2. **Some response:** this is a usual reaction if your entry takes or looks like taking some business from existing suppliers. The usual reaction is to reduce selling prices and so erode margins, the theory being that more established businesses can survive on lower margins. Your business plan should demonstrate that you can survive on lower margins for long enough for competitors to abandon this strategy. We

look at this approach in Chapter 13 when we stress-test your business model.

3.   **Fight to the death:** some companies take no prisoners. A good way to recognise a sector where competition will be cut throat is to see where advertising budgets are highest. Beer, mobile phones, motor vehicles and cosmetics are among the top five in terms of television spending. Your business plan needs to demonstrate that your product will be different in some material way, or that you have a barrier to entry such as some important IP. These are topics we will look at in Chapters 5 and 6.

In my experience

Nick Jenkins, Moonpig

"What I didn't want to do was to go head to head with an existing high street product at a lower margin as so many dotcoms seemed to be doing. This model was too easy to copy, meaning that competitors could easily enter my market, the result being that the cheapest would win, making it an unattractive business venture."

Estimating what new players could enter the market

When you enter a market you may unintentionally be sending a signal to others that there is a profitable market worth trying for. The threat of new entrants will be highest where the cost of getting into the market is relatively low and there is little in terms of regulation or intellectual property protection to prevent them.

Once you are in business then the most likely new entrants are your own employees who either want to emulate your success or who are frustrated by your inability to see opportunities quite as you do.

In my experience

Edwina Dunn and Clive Humby, dunnhumby

This is a classic example of a new entrant to market that one existing supplier could have predicted and prevented. While working at CACI, a leading market analysis company, Clive and Edwina came up with their vision to use data in a different way. This involved retaining and analysing customer data based on behaviour, which would enable companies to deliver marketing that was more relevant to their customers. They approached their employer with the idea but they were not willing to invest their profits in this new concept. Clive was adamant this idea should be pursued and his disappointment in the company's lack of vision led him to resign from the business in order to pursue the vision on his own. As Edwina, who was married to him, recalls, "I was literally fired 10 minutes later as they felt I would be competing with their business." She received a substantial payout – enough to dissuade her from claiming unfair dismissal. The result was a new player in the market, dunnhumby, which left CACI playing catch-up in a market they could have dominated from the outset.

Checklist

☑ List and briefly describe the businesses with which you will be competing directly.

☑ Analyse their size, profitability and operating methods, as far as you can.

☑ Describe their relative strengths and weaknesses compared both with each other and with your business.

☑ Think about where your products and those of your direct competitors fit on the Perceptual Map.

☑ Identify both your direct and indirect competitors and consider how you think they will react when you enter the market.

☑ Consider what substitutes are or could be available to your customers that might draw them away from your product.

☑ Think about who could follow you into the market and build that into your business plan, with particular emphasis on how you will defend your position.

☑ Consider ways to lock in employees with sufficient talent or expertise to set up in business against you. Share options, bonuses or allowing them to set up a separate division within your business are ways to create a win/win situation.

↻ CHAPTER 5

Getting your core strategy right

📖 What's in this chapter?

Businesses that start or expand without a business plan have by definition put little or no effort into shaping a strategy. Even those starting out with a business plan usually skip over the strategy section, or at best include a paragraph or two on their superiority, difference or that they will be first to market. The bulk of their business plan comprises details on how they will operate, market, finance and manage – all worthy and important tasks, but ones that will be reduced in effectiveness without a well thought out strategy.

In this chapter we'll cover:

→ why being first to market isn't always best
→ understanding why market share matters
→ appreciating the options
→ avoiding the 'muddled middle'
→ identifying the critical success factors.

Why being first to market isn't always best

Getting 'first mover advantage' describes what a business's strategy is and why it will succeed, even against the odds. This concept is one of the most enduring in business theory and practice. Research from the 1980s showed that market pioneers had advantages in distribution and market share, so business schools endorsed entrepreneurs and established businesses in their race to be first.

However beguiling the theory of first mover advantage is, it is probably wrong. Gerard Tellis, of the University of Southern California, and Peter Golder, of New York University's Stern business school, argued in their book *Will and Vision: How latecomers grow to dominate markets* (2001, McGraw-Hill Inc, USA), and in their subsequent academic research, that previous studies on the subject were deeply flawed. In the first instance, earlier studies were based on surveys of surviving companies and brands, excluding all the pioneers that failed. This helps some companies to look as though they were first to market even when they were not. Procter & Gamble (P&G) boasts that it created America's disposable-nappy (diaper) business. In fact, a company called Chux launched its product a quarter of a century before P&G entered the market in 1961.

Also, the questions used to gather much of the data in earlier research were at best ambiguous, and perhaps dangerously so. For example, 'one of the pioneers in first developing such products or services' was used as a proxy for 'first to market'. The authors emphasise their point by listing popular misconceptions of who were the real pioneers across the 66 markets they analysed. Online book sales – Amazon (wrong), Books.com (right); Copiers – Xerox (wrong), IBM (right); PCs – IBM/Apple (both wrong), Micro Instrumentation Telemetry Systems (MITS) introduced its PC the Altair, a $400 kit, in 1974 followed by Tandy Corporation (Radio Shack) in 1977.

First mover advantage should be thought of as a prelude to a business plan, rather than the plan itself. Certainly it's important to move with speed when an opportunity presents itself, but caution and assembling the resources – money, people and information – are vital for the advantage to be realised and built upon. In fact the most compelling evidence from all the research on the subject is that nearly half of all businesses pursuing a first to market strategy are fated to fail, while those following fairly close behind were three times as likely to succeed. Tellis and Golder claim the best strategy is to enter the market several years after pioneers, learn from their mistakes, benefit from their product and market development and so be more certain about customer preferences.

> **Startups Tip**
>
> Don't rely on first mover advantage alone as the way to explain why you will succeed. Decide on a strategic focus and show how you will learn quickly from your customers exactly what they expect you to deliver.

Understanding why market share matters

The relevant market will be shared by various competing businesses in different proportions. Typically there will be a market leader, a couple of market followers and a host of businesses trailing in their wake. The slice each competitor has of a market is its market share. You will find that marketing people are fixated on market share, perhaps even more so than on absolute sales. That may appear little more than a rational desire to beat the 'enemy' and appear higher in rankings, but it has a more deep-seated and profound logic.

Figure 5.1 over the page shows the market share and profitability of UK supermarkets at the year ending June 2011. Tesco, the market leader, made over twice as much profit per percentage point of market share as Morrisons. Any company capturing a sizeable share of their relevant market (see Chapter 3 for an explanation of relevant market) will have an implied cost advantage over any competitor with a smaller market share. That cost advantage can then be used to make more profit, lower prices and compete for an even greater share of the market, or to invest in making the product better, so stealing a march on competitors.

Back in the 1960s, management consultants observed a consistent relationship between the cost of producing an item (or delivering a

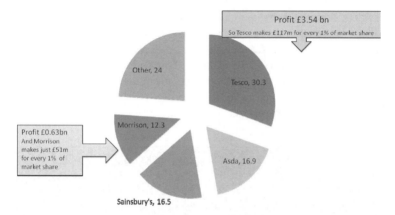

Figure 5.1 Market share, UK supermarkets June 2011

service) and the total quantity produced over the life of the product concerned. They noticed that total unit costs (labour and materials) fell by between 20% and 30% for every doubling of the cumulative quantity produced. The Boston Consulting Group (BCG) popularised the process with its experience curve (see Figure 5.2), which showed that each time the cumulative volume of doing something – either making a product or delivering a service – doubled, the unit cost dropped by a constant and predictable amount. The reasons for the cost drop include:

⇢ repetition makes people more familiar with tasks and consequently faster

⇢ more efficient materials and equipment become available from suppliers themselves as their costs go down through the experience curve effect

⇢ organisation, management and control procedures improve

⇢ engineering and production problems are solved.

Figure 5.2 shows that for the reasons outlined above, the unit cost of the product or service drops from 10 when only two have been produced, to around six when eight have been produced. That gives the supplier an advantage of four (40%) over any competitor languishing with an output of two.

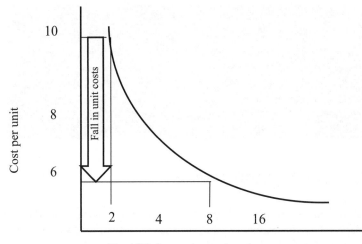

Figure 5.2 The experience curve

The important thing to remember here is that the product/market is as narrow as any discrete customer group you want to capture. Apple's iPad, for example, although a computer that covers some of the space occupied by netbooks and tablets, also straddles the entertainment arena once dominated by Archos. That makes it essentially a new category with a new cost curve and Apple has the lead market share, holding around 70%, well ahead of LG, BlackBerry Playbook, Motorola Zoom, HTC Flyer and Dell Streak, to name just a few. Apple uses the extra profit it makes from having the biggest market share to support innovation, while maintaining a premium price: a good example of a business having a lower unit cost than its competitors, while keeping prices high.

It's not just in the high tech or new product arena that experience counts. P&G, the leader in the household care and beauty and grooming markets, has 50 brands that are among some of the world's best-known household names – and which together make up 90% of its sales and more than 90% of profits. Twenty-three of those brands each generate more than $1 billion in annual sales and are in the top two positions in their respective markets.

> ## ⟲ Startups Tip
> Every industry has a different experience curve, which itself varies over time. You can find out more about how to calculate the curve for your industry on the Management And Accounting Web (www.maaw.info/LearningCurveSummary.htm) website; the National Aeronautics and Space Agency website (http://cost.jsc.nasa.gov/learn. html) provides a learning curve calculator.

Appreciating the options

Michael Porter, the Harvard Business School professor mentioned in Chapter 2, observed that two factors above all influenced a business's chances of making superior profits.

First, there was the attractiveness or otherwise of the industry in which it primarily operated, this we looked at in Chapter 2. Second, and in terms of an organisation's sphere of influence more importantly, was how the business positioned itself within that industry. In that respect a business could only have a cost advantage in that it could make product or deliver service for less than others. Or it could be different in a way that mattered to consumers, so that their offers would be unique, or at least relatively so. Porter added a further twist to his prescription. Businesses could follow either a cost advantage path or a differentiation path industry wide, or they could take a third path – they could concentrate on a narrow specific segment either with cost advantage or differentiation. This he termed 'focus' strategy.

These generic options were those most likely to let a business improve its share of the market, secure lower costs and so make superior profits, that in turn would make the business stronger still: in effect creating a virtuous circle.

Cost leadership

Low cost should not be confused with low price. A business with low costs may or may not pass those savings onto customers. Alternatively, they could use that position alongside tight cost controls and low margins to create an effective barrier to others considering either entering or extending their penetration of that market. Low-cost strategies are most likely to be achievable in large markets requiring large-scale capital investment, where production or service volumes are high and economies of scale can be achieved from long runs.

Low relative costs are not a lucky accident; they can be achieved by both big and small businesses through the following main activities.

- → **Operating efficiencies:** new processes, methods of working or less costly ways of working. Ryanair and easyJet are examples where analysing every component of the business made it possible to strip out major elements of cost – meals, free baggage and allocated seating for example – while leaving the essential proposition (we will fly you from A to B) intact.

- → **Product redesign:** this involves rethinking a product or service proposition fundamentally to look for more efficient ways to work or cheaper substitute materials to work with. The motor industry has adopted this approach with 'platform sharing', where major players including Citroen, Peugeot and Toyota have rethought their entry car models to share major components. In 2010, IKEA designers found a way to pack their popular bright red 'Ektorp' three-seater more compactly, doubling the amount of sofa they could cram into a given space. That shaved €100 from the price tag.

- → **Product standardisation:** a wide range of product and service offers claiming to extend customer choice invariably leads to higher costs. The challenge is to be sure that proliferation gives real choice and adds value. In 2008, the UK railway network took a long hard look at its dozens of different fare structures and scores of names (often for identical price structures) that had remained largely unchanged since the 1960s and reduced them to three basic product propositions, reducing cost of sale.

- → **Economies of scale:** this can be achieved only by being big or bold. The same head office, warehousing network and distribution chain can support Tesco's 4,000 stores as it can, say, the 2,400 that the Co-Operative Group has. The former will have a lower cost base by virtue of having more outlets to spread its costs over, as well as having more purchasing power.

Differentiation

Differentiation doesn't have to be confined to just the marketing arena, nor does it always lead to success if the subject of that differentiation goes out of fashion without much warning. Northern Rock, the failed bank that had to be nationalised to stay in business, thought its strategy of raising most of the money it lent out in mortgages through the money markets was a sure winner. It allowed the bank to grow faster than its competitors which placed more reliance on depositors for their funds. As long as interest rates were low and the money market functioned smoothly, it worked: but once the differentiators that fuelled its growth were reversed, its business model failed.

 In my experience

Mary and Doug Perkins, Specsavers

"We built up a high standing in the community by delivering great service and by being nice to people. It sounds simple, but this actually provided a key point of difference to the competition. Opticians at this time had a reputation for being standoffish."

Focus

Focused strategy involves concentrating on serving a particular market or a defined geographical region. IKEA, for example, targets young white-collar workers as its prime customer segment, selling through more than 200 stores in more than 30 countries. Ingvar Kamprad, an entrepreneur from the Småland province in southern Sweden, who founded the business in the late 1940s, offers home furnishing products of good function and design at prices young people can afford. He achieves this by using simple cost-cutting solutions that do not affect the quality of products.

Warren Buffett, the world's richest man, who knows a thing or two about focus, combined with Mars to buy US chewing gum manufacturer Wrigley for $23 billion (£11.6 billion) in May 2008. Chicago-based Wrigley, which launched its Spearmint and Juicy Fruit gums in the 1890s, has specialised in chewing gum ever since and consistently outperformed its more diversified competitors. Wrigley is the only major consumer products company to grow comfortably faster than the population in its markets and above the rate of inflation. Over the past decade or so, for example, other consumer products companies have diversified. Gillette moved into the batteries used to drive many of its products by acquiring Duracell. Nestlé bought Ralston Purina, Dreyer's, Ice Cream Partners, and Chef America. Both have trailed Wrigley's performance.

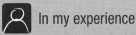 In my experience

Mary and Doug Perkins, Specsavers

"One of the key lessons I learnt was the importance of setting yourself apart from the competition by establishing unique selling points (USPs). As a new business, there was no point in merely copying a major player – you had to offer customers something different."

Avoiding the 'muddled middle'

On 6 January 2009, the last of the 813 Woolworths' stores that had operated for the best part of a century in the UK closed its doors for the last time. At one level this could just have been a story about another victim of the prevailing credit crunch, but Woolworths' problems pre-date that. The company's last annual report claimed its strength lay in the chain's focus on "the home, family and entertainment". But customer research indicated that it had no unique qualities, just an incoherent layout, with sun lotion next to the sweet counter, which in turn was next to the school bags, calendars, tools and clothes pegs. Customers tended to go there mostly as a last resort when the shops they usually used had run out of these products.

What finally killed off Woolworths was that it had become two quite different businesses: the high street retailer everyone knew and loved but bought very little from; and through Entertainment UK (EUK), another arm of its business, it was also a major supplier of CDs and DVDs to Asda, Marks & Spencer, Zavvi and for a while it had a lucrative contract to supply Tesco. The two businesses had very different cashflow profiles. The stores took credit from suppliers and cash from customers. The more they sold the more cash they generated. EUK's business model was the opposite, paying suppliers in 30 days but getting paid itself in 60 days or longer as the giant retailers used their buying muscle to take extended credit. The more EUK sold the worse Woolworths' cash position became. The deteriorating state of the economy meant that over the summer of 2008 most of Woolworths' 20 credit insurers stopped insuring its suppliers. This in turn meant Woolworths had to pay suppliers pro forma (up front) before the goods had been sold, consuming an additional £200 million and in effect wiping out cashflow reserves; for Woolworths, being in the muddled middle proved fatal.

> **Startups Tip**
> A small or new business should concentrate its efforts on pursuing a single strategic option: focus, differentiation or cost.

Identifying the critical success factors

While your business plan will include details on the thinking behind which strategic option you have chosen, at the end of the day your customers will chose you over competitors for a handful of reasons only. These CSFs are in effect the four or five things (aside from price, as you always have to offer value for money) that you have to get right with your product/service offer to succeed.

For example, if you were planning to open a greeting card business, a bricks-and-mortar version say of Moonpig, then location, range of cards, regular opening hours, knowledgeable staff and a pleasant environment could be the deciding factors for most potential customers.

> **Startups Tip**
> One way to arrive at CSFs is to ask yourself what you do and do not like about your competitors' businesses.

Pimlico Plumbers' founder, Charlie Mullins, makes this comment: "I've seen a lot of what goes wrong in the industry, what the customer doesn't like – they don't like a plumber turning up late, so we make sure ours don't and book appointments. They don't like a scruffy plumber; we make sure ours are not scruffy. They don't like dirty old vans; we don't have dirty old vans. People don't like answer machines or pressing numbers on phones – they want to talk to people. So we have a 24 hour call centre – someone will always answer the phone. So it's an opposite effect. Once you understand what the customer's needs are, and what they don't like, we've got a system in place to give them the complete opposite to what they were expecting. It's nothing that complicated."

You need to identify the CSFs for your product/service, rank their importance by, say, allocating them a share of 100%, then score yourself and your competitors. In the example in Table 5.1 over the page you can see that location is considered the most important factor and accounts for 40% of the reason to buy this type of product. Your competitor scores well on location, getting 4 out of a possible 5. By multiplying the score by the importance you arrive at the weighted score: 1.6. Continuing in the same way you can see that your total weighted score is 4.0 and your competitor's is 2.8, giving you a distinct superiority in terms of your product/service offer.

Of course, there is no easy way to arrive at exact figures for this table. Initially you will have to rely on your own judgement and the opinions of family and friends. Later, however, you can ask your customers using market research.

TABLE 5.1: *Assessing competitive advantage*

CSF factor	Importance (%)	Competitor score (0–5)	Weighted score	Your score (0–5)	Weighted score
Location	40	4	1.6	3	1.2
Range of cards	20	4	0.8	4	0.8
Knowledgeable staff	20	1	0.2	5	1.0
Opening hours	10	1	0.1	5	0.5
Pleasant environment	10	1	0.1	5	0.5
Total	100		2.8		4.0

🡒 Startups Tip

A new entrant to a market needs a significant advantage over established players – superior quality, service or faster delivery for example – otherwise customers will just look for a price. If your CSFs don't appear at first to give you a significant advantage over your competitors you need to think about what you can do to improve your competitive position. You could get a steer from Charlie Mullins (see previous page).

Checklist

- ✓ If you are expecting to be first to market, consider what other advantages for your proposition you can expand on in your business plan.

- ✓ Establish (roughly) the market shares of your key competitors.

- ✓ Describe the strategic direction being pursued by the business you are/will be competing with – focus, differentiation, cost.

- ✓ Identify any candidates in your market for the muddled middle.

- ✓ List the CSFs for your business area.

✎ *CHAPTER 6*

Your USP (unique selling proposition)

📖 What's in this chapter?

Chances are the executive summary (see Chapter 16 for more on this subject), a one- or two-page section of your business plan, is all that will be read before an investor, lender, prospective partner or key employee makes up their mind if your ideas make good business sense. That may sound harsh, but unless the executive summary sounds compelling, your plan will be pushed to get past the mail-room. The same rule applies for the handful of identifying factors that make up the tip of your identity iceberg – the bits the customer sees first. Markets are busy places and you have to have a distinctive proposition to stand out from the crowd.

Getting your strategy right, although essential for success, is not sufficient. You have to be able to communicate the value your proposition will represent for customers, succinctly and powerfully.

In this chapter we'll cover:

→ your business's place in the market: what are the USPs?

→ deciding on your business name

→ creating vision, values and mission statements

→ setting your business objectives

→ deciding on your personal goals

→ branding/image

→ identifying and registering intellectual property (IP).

Your business's place in the market: what are the USPs?

The term USP has several related meanings including 'uniquely serious problem' and 'unique selling proposition'. There are also a couple of variants such as 'unique competitive position' (UCP) and 'unique positioning proposition' (UPP). They are all ways to describe what makes your business stand out from the crowd.

Though the term is synonymous with the idea of a slogan or strapline that captures the value of the product in the mind of the user, it doesn't necessarily have to be so. Its purpose is to position your product against competitors in a manner that is hard to emulate or dislodge. For example, when Tim Waterstone started his bookshop chain in the UK the competition sold books in rows stacked on shelves, spine out in alphabetical order, sectioned off by subject. Bookshops operated a leisurely 9–5 existence, Monday to Friday and mornings only on Saturdays, staffed by assistants with no real understanding of books.

Waterstone's business USP addressed several major problems for his customers. In the first place, book buyers are usually in a job; were they not they would use a library; so not being open on evenings or weekends effectively constrained customers to a quick visit, sacrificing part, if not their entire, lunch break. The second problem concerned the way that people browse for books. Research shows that nearly two-thirds of book purchases are unplanned in the sense that the customer either had no firm idea of what they were looking for, or they simply stumbled across an appealing title while in the shop. With this in mind, books had to be distributed around the shop to maximise the opportunities for customers to stumble across an interesting title. While the spine out bookshelf layout was highly economic in terms of floor space and stockholding, it was both unappealing and a further factor limiting sales prospects. The third problem that Waterstone addressed was to staff his bookshops with people who could offer advice and information on authors and their books. He set out to create an environment that would appeal to literate young graduates rather than to barely articulate shop assistants. The Waterstone USP was its operating model.

Some companies have developed a catchy phrase or strapline that stakes out their unique position in the corporate landscape. "*Vorsprung Durch Technik*" (progress through technology) for Audi is an example of this approach. Another strategy is to set out to own the word that sums up the essence of your USP and turn it into an adjective. Hoover for vacuum cleaners and FedEx for overnight delivery are examples of this approach.

> ⌐ **Startups Tip**
> Being different from the competition is a powerful message, particularly if that difference solves a recognised problem.

These are the three ingredients of a successful USP:

1. **Unique:** although you may doubt it at first, customers care less about your product or service being either the best or the cheapest. Neither of those attributes is as easy as it seems to measure or recognise. It's the two or three biggest benefits of owning your product or doing business with you that is where your uniqueness must lie. You must show why those benefits are important to them, and how you will deliver. FedEx used "When it Absolutely, Positively has to be there overnight", as their unique benefit for two decades, only comparatively recently changing that to "The World On Time".

2. **Selling:** this involves getting people to part with their cash. John Lewis, for example, has "never knowingly undersold" as its powerful message to consumers that they can safely set price considerations to one side when they come to making their choice, and just get right on and buy.

3. **Proposition:** to be compelling you need to show you are solving a problem or pain point for your customer. Domino's Pizza decided for their customers the pain point was waiting so they adopted "Pizza delivered in 30 minutes or it's free" as their proposition. In 2009, they backed this up with an online 'Domino's tracker', keeping customers informed of their order status to the point of despatch.

In my experience

Edwina Dunn and Clive Humby, dunnhumby

"Having a unique selling point is a must for any new business, but offering a completely new service also has its downsides: there is nothing to compare our business to so it was a challenge setting both budgets and expectations."

Deciding on your business name

A good name, in effect, can become a one- or two-word summary of your business strategy. Jeff Bezos originally chose 'Cadabra' as the name for his business (as in abracadabra), summing up the magic of being able to find any book online. After a few phone calls to canvas opinions he ditched Cadabra as it was too easily confused with 'cadaver'! He settled on Amazon, figuring that most people thought it to be the largest river in the world and he wanted to convey the image of having the "Earth's Biggest Book Store".

Google, though a colossally successful venture, struggled to arrive at a meaningful business name. They started with 'BackRub', as their algorithms checked backlinks to estimate the importance of a site, but moved onto use Google, a misspelling of the word 'googol', the number one followed by one hundred zeros, chosen to convey the idea of large quantities of information being sifted for useful data. It's unlikely that many people outside of the Stanford University campus where the founders developed their business idea would have any idea what a googol was (or why it would help describe the biggest search engine), but at the time geeks populated the internet and the name caught on.

> ### Startups Tip
> Don't choose a name that could restrict future growth. Amazon is a generic name that can be applied to any product or service. Bezos quickly replaced "Earth's Biggest Book Store" with the tagline "Books, Music and More".

Your business name is almost always the first way people get to hear about your venture. So unless it conveys your essence quickly and clearly, you could have an uphill struggle on your hands. Once you have to start explaining what you do, the job of communicating gets harder.

A business name can, in effect, be the starting and sustaining point in differentiating you from your competitors and, as such, should be carefully chosen, be protected by trademarks where possible (see later in this chapter) and be written in a distinctive way. It follows, therefore, that the main consideration in choosing a business name is its commercial usefulness.

When you choose a business name, you are also choosing an identity, so it should reflect:

⇢ who you are

⇢ what you do

⇢ how you do it.

> ### Startups Tip
> Given all the marketing investment you will make in your business name, you should check with a trademark agent whether you can protect your chosen name (descriptive words, surnames and place names are not normally allowed except after long use).

There are some 80–90 controlled names, which include words such as 'international', 'bank' and 'royal'. Anyone wanting to use a 'controlled' name will have to get permission. This is simply to prevent a business implying that it is something that it is not.

Businesses that intend to trade under names other than those of their owner(s) must state who does own the business and how the owner can be contacted. So, if you are a sole trader or partnership (see Chapter 12 for more on this subject), and you only use surnames with or without forenames or initials, you are not affected. Companies are also not affected if they simply use their full corporate name.

> ### Startups Tip
> Check out Startups (www.startups.co.uk/naming-your-business) for everything you need to know about choosing a name for your business.

If any name other than the 'true' name is to be used, then you must disclose the name of the owner(s) and an address in the UK to which business documents can be sent. This information has to be shown on all business letters, orders for goods and services, invoices and receipts, and statements and demands for business debts. Also, a copy has to be displayed prominently on all business premises.

If you are setting up as a limited company you will have to submit your choice of name to the Companies Registration Office along with the other documents required for registration. It will be accepted unless there is another company with that name on the register, or the Registrar considers the name to be obscene, offensive or illegal.

> ### In my experience
>
> ### Edwina Dunn and Clive Humby, dunnhumby
>
> "We chose to combine our surnames – Dunn and Humby – to create our company name. We thought this through carefully. With around 10 years' experience of customer data between us, we felt it important to make the most of our reputations in the industry, and we thought it would help attract clients to our fledgling business."

Names on the web

If you plan to have an internet presence, you will need a domain name. That is a name by which your business is known on the internet and lets people find you by entering your name into their browser address box. Ideally, you want a domain name that is as close as possible to your business name, and which captures the essence of your business neatly so that you will come up readily on search engines.

If you find your business name has already been grabbed by someone else, don't panic; at least not just yet. In June 2011, the Internet Corporation of Assigned Names and Numbers (ICAN), the non-profit group which controls the internet domain name system, announced guidelines on a new host of web addresses which will allow companies to purchase URLs ending in their business name rather than '.com', '.co.uk' etc.

If your business name is registered as a trademark (see later in this chapter) you may (as current case law develops) be able to prevent another business from using it as a domain name on the internet. Once you have decided on a selection of possible domain names, your internet service provider (ISP), the organisation that you use to link your computer to the internet, can submit a domain name application on your behalf.

In my experience

Nick Jenkins, Moonpig

"The reliance on word of mouth promotion above all is also at the heart of the company's name. I wanted a domain name that was easy to remember, and fun enough that customers would want to tell their friends about it. I was looking for a two syllable domain, but I couldn't find the right combination available and I didn't want to buy one from somebody else." Moonpig – Nick's school nickname – worked. At the time, if you entered it into Google nothing came up, and there was the added advantage that it lent itself well to a logo: it's easy enough to remember a pig in a space helmet.

Creating vision, value and mission statements

Your business plan sets out what business you are in, or going into, and how you will get there. Your plan will be reviewed as events unwind and revised as necessary from time to time. Maynard Keynes's view that 'when the facts change I change my mind' may well be valid but nothing is so debilitating to customers, suppliers, employees or financial backers as a business that appears to keep changing course. A well-founded business may well tack from time to time, but the general direction of travel should be set for the longer term in these three statements.

Vision

A vision is about stretching the organisation's reach beyond its grasp. Few now can see how the vision can be achieved, but can see that it would be great if it could be.

Microsoft's vision of a computer in every home, formed when few offices had one, is one example of a vision that has nearly been achieved. Started as a company goal back in 1990, it might have raised a wry smile; after all, it was only a few decades before then that IBM had estimated the entire world demand for its computers as seven! Their updated vision to "create experiences that combine the magic of software with the power of internet services across a world of devices", is rather less succinct! Apple, Microsoft's arch rival, has as its vision to "make things that make an impact". It does this by using the latest technology, investing in packaging and design, making its products easier to use and more elegant than anything else around, and then selling them at a premium price. Personal computers, music players, smartphones and tablet computers, and now cloud-based services, have all been treated to the Apple visionary touch with considerable success. In 2011, Apple overtook Microsoft in terms of its stock market value.

IBM's vision is to package technology for use by businesses. Starting out with punch-card tabulators, IBM adapted over its 100 plus-year history to supplying magnetic-tape systems, mainframes, PCs, and consulting, since it bought the consulting arm of PricewaterhouseCoopers, an accounting firm, in 2002. Building a business around a vision, rather than a specific product or technology, makes it easier to get employees, investors and customers to buy into a long-term commitment to a business, seeing they could have opportunities for progression in an organisation that knows where it is going.

Mission

A mission is a direction statement, intended to focus your attention on the essentials that encapsulate your specific competence(s) in relation to the market/customers you plan to serve. First, the mission should be narrow enough to give direction and guidance to everyone in the business. This concentration is the key to business success because it is only by focusing on specific needs that a small business can differentiate itself from its larger competitors. Nothing kills off a business faster than trying to do too many different things too soon. Second, the mission should open up a large enough market to allow the business to grow and realise its potential. You can always add a bit on later. In summary, the mission statement should explain the following.

-⇢   What business you are in and your purpose.

-⇢   What you want to achieve over the next one to three years, ie your strategic goal.

Above all, mission statements must be realistic, achievable – and brief.

Toys R Us has as its mission "To be the world's greatest kids' brand"; Starbucks's mission is "To inspire and nurture the human spirit – one person, one cup and one neighbourhood at a time". Neither of those missions say anything about products or services, rather they are focused on customer groups – kids for Toys R Us and on needs for Starbucks, both areas likely to be around for a while yet.

In my experience

Mary and Doug Perkins, Specsavers

"I had a clear vision of how opticians could operate in order to deliver better value, choice and transparency to consumers. Driven by our mission to provide affordable eye care to all, we built the company around the idea of treating others respectfully. Some 25 years later we still describe our billion pound international company as a family-owned business with family values."

Values

A business faces tough choices every day, and the bigger it gets the greater the number of people responsible for setting out what you ultimately stand for – profits alone, or principled profits.

Defining your values will make it possible for everyone working for you to know how to behave in any situation. Southwest Airlines, the first (and arguably the best) low-cost airline has cultivated a reputation for being the 'nice' airline. A past CEO, James Parker, tells a story that sums up their values – "We want people to consistently do the right thing because they want to." One evening a flight landed in Detroit and all the passengers, bar one, a young girl, disembarked. She should have got off at Chicago, an earlier stop, but failed to do so. Despite this being the night before Thanksgiving, the pilot and crew knew that they had to get the passenger back to her anxious parents. Without asking for company permission, they just took off and returned the girl to her correct destination. They knew what should be done, regardless of the additional cost and inconvenience, and just got on with it.

Toys R Us has what it calls its 'R' values: "At Toys R Us, Inc., we believe that by being rapid, real, reliable and responsible, we will best serve our customers, employees, shareholders, communities and kids!

→ Rapid: we believe that speed is a reflection of our culture. Our team is focused and clear with common, user-friendly processes and solutions; fast and urgent in decision-making and speed-to-market; and quick in adapting to change.

→ Real: our team is urgent, sincere, authentic, helpful to work with and confident. We are 'playing to win!'

→ Reliable: being reliable means working as a team so everything can move faster. We are a company that is dependable, and we produce what we promise.

→ Responsible: we believe that honesty, integrity and compassion are the foundation upon which we work together and conduct our business. Keeping kids safe is a cornerstone of the brand.

"As a company, and as individuals, we value integrity, honesty, openness, personal excellence, constructive self-criticism, continual self-improvement, and mutual respect. We are committed to our customers and partners and have a passion for technology. We take on big challenges, and pride ourselves on seeing them through. We hold ourselves accountable to our customers, shareholders, partners, and employees by honouring our commitments, providing results, and striving for the highest quality."

In my experience

Mary and Doug Perkins, Specsavers

"The company remains totally committed to the 'family values' ethos and treating others as you wish to be treated. This was formalised in 2008 when Specsavers signed up to a global ethical trading policy. The business also supports numerous charities. Since its foundation in 1985, Vision Aid Overseas has worked in 26 countries and helped over one million patients to see."

Setting your business objectives

The milestones on the way to realising the vision and mission are measured by the achievement of business objectives. Your business plan should set out the primary goals in terms of profit, turnover and business value, particularly if you want to attract outside investment. Pizza Express, for example, set out its goals in June 2011 as aiming to nearly double their number of outlets from 318 to 700 by 2020. Majestic Wine announced a similar sounding goal, aiming to add 12 new stores a year for the next 10 years.

Make sure that your business plan contains SMART objectives.

- **Specific:** relates to specific tasks and activities, not general statements about improvements.
- **Measurable:** it should be possible to assess whether or not they have been achieved.
- **Attainable:** it should be possible for the employee to achieve the desired outcome.
- **Realistic:** within the employee's current or planned-for capability.
- **Timed:** to be achieved by a specific date.

Deciding on your personal goals

At the end of the day, your business plan has to show what you expect to achieve by realising the goals set for your business. This could be creating a venture that will give your family work; give you a lifetime's challenge; provide an opportunity to build a valuable business that can be sold on – all are some possible personal aims. Although your business plan is focused on strategic long-term action, as the Chinese proverb says: "the longest journey starts with a single step".

The late Stephen Covey, best known for his book *The 7 Habits of Highly Effective People* (Simon & Schuster, 2004), devotes two of the habits to personal goals. The first of these is "start with the end in mind". Here Covey recommends developing a personal mission statement and acquiring what he calls the habit of personal leadership so that you can keep steering in the right direction despite changing circumstances. Developing this habit allows you to concentrate most of your energies on activities relevant to your end goal, avoid distractions and in the process become more productive and successful.

Secondly, he says "put first things first". The previous habit involves self-leadership, this one is about self-management. Leadership, Covey states, "decides what the first things are, and management is the discipline of carrying out your program". Covey also quotes Peter Drucker who pointed out that the expression 'time management' is something of a misnomer: "We have a constant amount of time, no matter what we do; the challenge we face is to manage ourselves. To be an effective manager of yourself, you must organise and execute around priorities."

Covey introduces the idea of tasks fitting into four quadrants, with important–not important on one continuum and urgent–not urgent on the other. Reports, meetings, calls, interruptions and the occasional genuine crisis will drag us into spending time in quadrants I and III in Figure 6.1. Time spent on quadrant IV activities is only for those determined to fail.

Covey recommends a way to up your time on quadrant II tasks.

Figure 6.1 Covey's four-quadrant time manager

⇢ Write down two or three important results you feel you should accomplish in the short term. At least some of these goals should be quadrant II activities.

⇢ Look at the next few weeks and months ahead with your goals in mind, and block out the time each day to achieve them. With your key goals locked in, see what time is left for everything else! How well you succeed will depend on how resilient and determined you are at defending your most important priorities.

Your business plan should include your personal goals and the way you will prioritise your time to ensure they are achieved.

Branding/image

Building a brand takes time and a considerable amount of effort to establish. Just putting a sentence into your business plan stating that you will "create a brand image", without showing why and how you will go about it, will significantly reduce a reader's confidence in your venture. Having a brand is considered the Holy Grail when it comes to creating a unique identity for a business. By creating brand value, that is the price premium commanded by a branded product over its unbranded or less appealing competitors, a business can end up with a valuable asset.

A brand encompasses not just what a product is or does but all the elements such as logo, symbols, image, reputation and associations. Branding is an intangible way of differentiating a business in a way that captures and retains markets through loyalty to that brand. Coca-Cola tastes little different from a supermarket brand, but the promotion that supports the brand confers on the consumer the chance to share the attractive life style of those 'cool' people in the adverts. Apple's iPod is differentiated from just any old MP3 player in much the same way. Intel and Audi are examples of branding designed to reassure consumers in unfamiliar territory that a product will deliver. Body Shop International exudes ethics and concern for the environment, where other cosmetics concentrate on how they will make the wearer look beautiful.

A brand generates trust, a fact that appears to transcend business sectors. According to BrandZ, consideration of brand in the purchase decision has risen by 20 percentage points since 2005, so in uncertain economic conditions people turn to something they can trust – an established brand. For example, over the period 2005–10 while companies in the S&P 500 lost 11.5% in value, those of the top 100 brands gained 18.5%.

> **Startups Tip**
> You can find out more about how to making branding work best for your business on the Startups website (www.startups.co.uk/branding).

Identifying and registering intellectual property (IP)

Your business plan should show that you have, or how you plan to acquire, ownership of any IP that is central to your business. Even if your business is not highly technical or stashed full of innovations, if your logo, slogan or the design of your product is part of your uniqueness that differentiates you from others in the market, you will want to make sure some newcomer can't step in and help themselves to your valuable asset.

You should investigate the four categories of protection: patenting, which protects 'how something works'; trademark registration, which protects 'what something's called'; design registration, which protects 'how something looks'; and copyright, which protects 'work on paper, film and DVD'. Some products may be covered by two or more categories, eg the mechanism of a clock may be patented while its appearance may be design registered.

Each category requires a different set of procedures, offers a different level of protection and extends for a different period of time. They all have one thing in common, though: in the event of any infringement your only redress is through the courts, and going to law can take time and money, whether you win or lose; so you should consider insuring against such eventualities.

King of Shaves founder, Will King, launched his razor against Gillette using IP advantage to carve out a niche. He wasn't daunted at being up against a giant: "There's nothing better than dealing with a strong one because strong competitors are in markets that are really quite useful to be in – ie, they're big. Now what you clearly can't do is copy the strong competitor because all you'll get is what he leaves you to be eaten and you're just doing the same as he's doing, so if we'd chosen to 'copy' Gillette we'd have probably created a 17-blade razor with two batteries in it, raised £200m from venture capital and tried to spend it, lost all of the money and gone bust. We haven't done that. What we have done though is recognise the fact that great products need a very strong innovation platform. Now, we're only talking about shaving men's stubble without cutting yourself here – sounds quite simple, but the engineering piece in it is really quite edgy, no pun intended. There's a lot of technology in it, a lot of tolerance issues, a lot of patents in there, a lot of prior art out there. Big competitors are out there. They've got big because they're good, but maybe sometimes the bigger they are, the harder they fall because of the lack of competition they've faced."

Whether you have developed an original product, designed a memorable and eye-catching company logo or built up a trusted and well-known brand, you need to be aware of the importance of IP. The Startups website (www.startups.co.uk/intellectual-property) covers everything from patents to trademarks and copyright, and offers advice on what to do if you feel your IP rights have been infringed.

You can also get comprehensive information, help and advice on matters relating to IP from the UK Intellectual Property Office (www.ipo.gov.uk), which has all the information needed to patent, trademark, copyright or register a design, and for information on international intellectual property, see the European Patent Office (www.epo.org), US Patent and Trade Mark Office (www.uspto.gov) and the World Intellectual Property Association (www.wipo.int).

Checklist

☑ List your customers' biggest frustrations in buying the type of product or service you offer.

☑ Describe the two or three most important benefits you offer to your customers.

☑ List five possible names for your business; rank them in order of preference and explain why you have chosen that order.

☑ Identify your three most important business objectives.

☑ Set out the personal goals that you expect to achieve from achieving your business plan.

↵ CHAPTER 7

The marketing plan

📖 What's in this chapter?

Marketing is the heart without which no business can function, however clever or timely its business proposition. It is the process that ensures the right products and services get to the right markets at the right time and at the right price. As such it is the centrepiece of every business plan. The ingredients with which marketing strategy can be developed and implemented are known as the marketing mix. This comprises the four Ps: price, product (or/and service), promotion and place. A fifth 'P', people, is often added. Just as with cooking taking the same or similar ingredients in different proportions can result in very different 'products'.

In this chapter we'll cover:

→ *putting boundaries on your product/service offer*

- establishing a selling price: skim, penetrate and more
- establishing payment and other terms of trade
- deciding on an advertising and promotion strategy
- planning your route to market
- establishing a marketing budget.

Putting boundaries on your product/ service offer

The maternity wear business whose product features and benefits were listed in Table 3.1 (see p. 47) put this description in its business plan: "We make clothes for the mother to be that will allow them to still feel fashionably dressed." That is specific in one sense but still leaves a question mark over exactly what clothes they will be: dresses, sweatshirts, coats, skirts, jeans? Johnnie Boden started out with a hand-drawn catalogue containing just eight items. Too many products and your efforts could be spread too thin; too few and you could miss out on opportunities staring you in the face.

Is one product enough?

One-product businesses are the natural route for a new business, particularly those with a streak of innovation, but they are extremely vulnerable to competition, changes in fashion and technological obsolescence; having only one product can also limit the growth potential of the enterprise. A question mark must inevitably hang over such ventures until they can broaden out their product base into, preferably, a 'family' of related products or services.

> ### Startups Tip
> For the purposes of your business plan, include only the products and services you expect to sell in the first year. A brief description of products that could be introduced later will be sufficient to show you have ideas for growth.

Defining your product/service offer

Even a single product has the potential for a number of variations that could be used to make it more attractive to different market segments (see Chapter 3 for more on market segments). At its simplest you could charge a premium price for a faster delivery (courier services) or a more comfortable journey (business class air travel). Majestic Wines had a single product offer – wine by the dozen. In 2010, it introduced a subtle change, offering half cases and in effect shifting the price point down, and its sales increased significantly. Your business plan should describe clearly the elements that will make up your product/service offer:

- ➼ after-sales service and support
- ➼ availability
- ➼ brand name/image
- ➼ colour/flavour/odour/touch
- ➼ delivery
- ➼ design
- ➼ packaging

- ➼ payment terms.
- ➼ performance and reliability
- ➼ presentation and appearance
- ➼ refund and returns policy
- ➼ safety
- ➼ size
- ➼ specification and functionality
- ➼ quality

Establishing a selling price: skim, penetrate and more

The single number that is the hardest to arrive at (and the most likely to be questioned by everyone reading your business plan) is the selling price. Though clearly a marketing decision, pricing cuts across almost every area of a business. Elasticity of demand, the economist's domain, comes into play from the outset. Set too high a price and no one buys; too low and your sales could go right off the scale, generating plenty of demand but very little profit. The accounts and production areas are concerned that sales will at least be sufficient to reach break-even in reasonable time.

You may also be concerned about the signals in terms of image that prices can send. However profitable a certain price may be for the business, it may just be so low that it devalues other products in your range. Apple, for example, has a position fairly and squarely at the premium end of the pricing scale. Its customers expect to pay high prices for the privilege of buying an exciting product.

Skim versus penetrate

Two generic pricing strategies need to be decided between before you can fine tune your business plans. Skimming involves setting a price at the high end of what you believe the market will bear. This would be a strategy to pursue if you had a very limited amount of product available for sale and would rather 'ration' than disappoint customers. It is also a way to target the 'innovators' in your market who are happy to pay a premium to be among the first to have a new product (see Chapter 3 for more on innovators). To be successful with this strategy you would need to be sure competitors can't just step in and soak up the demand that you have created.

Penetration pricing is the mirror image: prices are set at the low end, while being above your costs. Prices set so as to reduce your customer's need to shop around; slogans such as "everyday low prices" are used to emphasise this policy. The aim here is to grab as much of the market as you can before competitors arrive on the scene and so hopefully lock them out. The danger here is that you need a lot of volume either of product or hours sold before you can make a decent profit. This in turn means tying up more money for longer before you break even. Your business plan will have to show that this additional investment will pay off.

> **Startups Tip**
>
> It is an immutable law that raising prices is a whole lot more difficult than lowering them. It is less of a problem if the market as a whole is moving up, but raising a price because you set it too low in the first place is a challenge to say the least.

Value pricing

Another consideration when setting your prices is the value of the product or service in the customer's mind. His or her opinion of price may have little or no relation to the cost, and he or she may be ignorant of the price charged by the competition, especially if the product or service is a new one. In fact, many consumers perceive price as a reliable guide to the value they can expect to receive. The more you pay, the more you get. With this in mind, had Dyson launched his revolutionary vacuum cleaner, with its claims of superior performance, at a price below that of its peers, then some potential customers might have questioned those claims.

In its literature, Dyson cites as the inspiration for the new vacuum cleaner the inferior performance of existing products in the same price band. A product at six times the Dyson price is the one whose performance Dyson seeks to emulate. The image created is that, although the price is at the high end of general run-of-the-mill products, the performance is disproportionately greater. The runaway success of Dyson's vacuum cleaner would tend to endorse this argument.

In my experience

Mary and Doug Perkins, Specsavers

"When we launched, opticians were charging higher prices for stronger prescriptions. This didn't seem fair; I strongly believe that people should pay the same for their lenses no matter how bad their eyesight. Critics said it couldn't be done, but this was the system Specsavers introduced, and made a success."

Real-time pricing

Markets have always worked by trying to match current demand to current supply, using price as the balancing factor. The reason you can sell your shares in Marks & Spencer or Tesco any time the market is open is not because the businesses have suddenly become undesirable or risky. It's just that someone out there wants them more than you do.

The internet has made it possible for companies such as easyJet, a budget airline, to vary prices an infinite number of times each day. It prices to fill its planes, and you could pay anything from £30 to £200 (including airport taxes) for the same trip, depending on the demand for that flight. Ryanair, Eurotunnel and almost every hotel chain have similar price ranges based on the basic rule – discounted low fares for early reservations and full fares for desperate late callers!

Internet auction pricing

The theory of auctioning is simple. Have as many interested potential buyers as possible see an item, set a time limit for the transaction to be completed and let them fight it out. The highest bidder wins and, in general, you can get higher prices than by selling through traditional pricing strategies. eBay was a pioneer in the new auction house sector and is still perhaps the best known. But there are dozens of other auction houses you can plug into.

Pay what you like pricing

This strategy is based on the auction concept, but buyers set their own price. The twist is that there is no limit on supply, so everyone can have one at the price they want to pay. Radiohead, the band, released its seventh album *In Rainbows* in October 2007 as a download on its website where fans could pay what they wished from nothing to £99.99. Estimates by the online survey group comScore indicate that of the 1.2 million visitors to Radiohead's website three out of five downloaders paid nothing, the payers averaged £3 per album so allowing for the freeloaders the band realised £1.11 per album. The band reckoned that was more than they would have made in a traditional label deal. In fact the version of the album released in this way was not the definitive one, that was released three months later in CD format, debuting at number one in the USA and the UK. A number of restaurateurs are experimenting with this pricing strategy with some success, but as yet it is in its infancy.

In my experience

Mary and Doug Perkins, Specsavers

"A major problem we set out to solve was the lack of transparency on pricing. People needed to know what they were going to pay before they got to the till. Our prices were displayed on the frames and included the lenses; we called it Complete Price."

Establishing payment and other terms of trade

When and how you get paid is a vital input to your cashflow forecast (see Chapter 10), a major section in your business plan. As well as your pricing strategy you should explain in your business plan how you expect to get paid. One of the top three reasons that businesses fail is because a customer fails to pay up in full or on time. You should outline the steps that you will be taking to make sure this doesn't happen to your business.

Set your terms of trade

You need to decide on your terms and conditions of sale, and ensure they are printed on your order acceptance stationery. Terms should include when and how you require to be paid and under what conditions you will accept cancellations or offer refunds. The websites of the Office of Fair Trading (www.oft.gov.uk) and Trading Standards Central (www.tradingstandards.gov.uk) contain information on most aspects of trading relationships.

Check credit worthiness

There is a wealth of information on credit status for both individuals and businesses at prices from £5 for basic information through to £200 for a very comprehensive picture. So there is no need to trade unknowingly with individuals or businesses that pose a credit risk.

The major agencies that provide credit data on business and consumers include Experian (www.UKexperian.com), Dun & Bradstreet (www.dnb.com), Creditgate.com (www.creditgate.com) and Credit Reporting (www.creditreporting.co.uk). Between them they offer a comprehensive range of credit reports instantly online, including advice on credit limit and county court judgments (CCJs).

Visit the Institute of Credit Management and the Credit Management Research Centre's website (www.cmrc.co.uk/publications). There you can see the latest research on trade credit and the payment behaviour of different industry sectors.

Get a consumer credit licence

If you plan to let your customers buy on credit or hire out or lease products to private individuals or to businesses, then you will in all probability have to apply to be licensed to provide credit. If you think you may need to be licensed, see the regulations on the website of the Office of Fair Trading (www.oft.gov.uk).

Deciding on an advertising and promotion strategy

Advertising and promotion is often the woolliest section in a business plan. Often entrepreneurs feel that the subject is more art than science, but there are some tools that will help you be more certain of achieving your marketing objectives. The answers to the five questions given below should underpin this aspect of your business plan.

1. What do you want to happen?

2. If that happens, how much is it worth?

3. What message will make it happen?

4. What media will work best?

5. How will you measure the effectiveness of your effort and expense?

What do you want to happen?

What do you want potential customers to do to enable you to sell them your products? Do you want them to visit your website; phone, write or email you; return a card, or to send an order in the post? Do you expect them to have an immediate need to which you want them to respond now, or is it that you want them to remember you at some future date when they have a need for whatever it is you are selling?

The more you are able to identify a specific response in terms of orders, visits, phone calls or requests for literature, the better your promotional effort will be tailored to achieve your objective, and the more clearly you will be able to assess the effectiveness of your promotion and its cost versus its yield.

> ### Startups Tip
> Of all the marketing tools available to businesses, advertising is the most widely used, although it is often the least effective. Check out the Startups section on advertising (www.startups.co.uk/advertising), which explores the different advertising mediums and offers advice for small businesses on how to maximise the results of their advertising campaigns.

How much is that worth to you?

Once you know what you want a particular promotional activity to achieve, it becomes a little easier to estimate its cost. Putting a cost/benefit analysis into your business plan will show that you are treating these expenses as an investment; always a comfort to anyone putting money into a business. For example, if a £500 advertisement is expected to generate 50 enquiries for your product, and experience tells you that on average 10% of enquiries result in orders and your profit margin is £200 per product, then you can expect a £2,000 profit. That 'benefit' is much greater than the £500 cost of the advertisement and is likely to pay back even if you only get half the business projected.

> ### Startups Tip
> For press advertising, start off with the smallest that will fit your copy, for example one-sixteenth of a page. Then once the medium has proved itself, progress gradually either to a larger size or more frequent placings.

Measuring results

Include in your plan details of how you will measure results – sales, enquiries, requests for information, attendees at an exhibition or people coming through your shop door.

In my experience

Nick Jenkins, Moonpig

"Our first marketing campaign was pretty hit and miss; we tried a number of affiliate deals, some PR and invested in search engine optimisation. But none of these was as effective as the power of viral marketing. In fact, Moonpig's profile was effectively raised through word of mouth – people received a card, were taken by it, went online and ordered one for someone else."

Deciding the message

To answer this question you must look at your business and its products from the customer's standpoint and be able to answer the hypothetical question, "Why should I buy your product?" Your promotional message must be built around these factors and must consist of facts about the business and the product. The stress here is on the word 'fact', and while there may be many types of fact surrounding you and your product, your customers are only interested in two: the facts that influence their buying decisions, and the ways in which your business and its products stand out from the competition. These facts must be translated into benefits.

There is an assumption sometimes that everyone buys for obvious, logical reasons only, when we all know of innumerable examples showing this is not so. Do people only buy new clothes when the old ones are worn out? Do bosses have desks that are bigger than their subordinates' because they have more papers to put on them?

Choosing the media

Your market research should produce a clear understanding of who your potential customers are, which in turn will provide pointers as to how to reach them. But even when you know who you want to reach with your advertising message it's not always plain sailing. The *Golfing Times*, for example, will be effective at reaching golfers but less so at reaching their partners who might be persuaded to buy them equipment for Christmas or birthdays. Also the *Golfing Times* will be jam packed with competitors.

Table 7.1 provides an overview of media outlets you should investigate to help prepare your media plan.

TABLE 7.1: *Business plan advertising media plan*

Above the line (ATL) – impersonal mass media		Below the line (BTL) – personal targeted media	
Media	*Using?*	*Media*	*Using?*
TV, cinema and radio advertising		Direct mail – leaflets, flyers, brochures	
Print – newspapers, magazines, directories and classified ads		Direct email, viral marketing	
Internet banner ads etc		Sales promotions, including point of sales material	
Search engine optimisation and placing		Public relations (PR) including press releases, news stories, etc	
Podcasts		Letterheads, stationery and business cards	
Posters and billboards		Blogs, online communities and social networking sites	

PR guru Max Clifford reckons PR is a highly cost-effective way for a small business to get its message across. "When it works, PR is incredibly effective. Editorial is far more persuasive to most people than advertising. So I know from things that we've been involved with in years gone by, that from a small outlay, a business has taken off and made fortunes, because of what we were able to bring to the table very quickly and comparatively cheaply. Does it work for everyone? Well I'm sure it doesn't. But I think certainly if I were to reverse the roles, if I was about to launch a small business, it would be something that I would look at very very carefully because I know how effective it can be. You might need to spend £1 million on advertising to achieve what you could get, and get far better returns, from £100,000 of PR."

Planning your route to market

In my experience

Edwina Dunn and Clive Humby, dunnhumby

"To get our first customer we used our existing contacts list, approaching a few with a simple explanation of what we could offer and how it could impact on the business. Within two months we had found our first client."

How you are actually going to get customers to make their buying decisions is invariably high on any list of vital issues to be covered in your business plan. It is, in effect, the link between your strategy – what you will sell, to whom and why they should buy from you – and your financial forecasts that make up the centrepiece of any business plan. The essential relationship that has to be explained and measured is how much activity (and by inference cost) has to be incurred to achieve the level of sales required in your business plan. The main options and possible measures are listed in Table 7.2 over the page.

There are no hard and fast rules about which route to market is best. Dell, for example, sold direct through mailorder, the telephone and online for 23 years. In 2008, it changed strategy adding distribution through third-party retailers such as PC World and Tesco, to compete

TABLE 7.2: Routes to market

Route to market	Measurement	
Method	**Activity**	**Conversion Measure**
Retail outlet	Local daily/weekly footfall of potential customers	Percentage of those likely to buy and their average spend
Direct sales	Visits per salesperson per month/quarter	Call to order conversion rate multiplied by average order size
Sales agents/distributors	Number of appointed	Average orders per agent/ distributor
Online sales	Website hits	Buy to hit ratio multiplied by average spend
Offline direct sales – catalogues, leaflets, etc	Mailing volumes	Orders per 1,000 mailings multiplied by average order size

with HP, which had knocked it into second place. You just have to figure out where your target market is most likely to want to buy from you.

Conversion rates are equally difficult to arrive at. When Boden, the clothing retailer, saw declining response rates for enquirers on traditional mailings, they launched the 'Love Story' campaign featuring a personalised mailing, addressed to a customer's first name with a J Loves logo at the front. A fold-out spread was unique to each customer, based on their shopping history and life story with the brand. Overall results for this catalogue mailing delivered a near 30% uplift in response.

Startups Tip

However uncertain you are of conversion rates or average order size, you will have to put figures in for them in your business plan and explain how you arrived at them.

If you are new to this business area, then talk to someone knowledgeable in the sector. Pick someone you won't be competing against.

A conversion rate is the percentage of potential customers that your marketing effort will reach who take the action that you want. In your business plan you should explain how you arrived at that rate and what your average order size will be.

> ### Startups Tip
> In today's ever-changing world, online marketing has an increasingly important role. Boosting your reputation is vital for any business, and the Startups section on this topic (www.startups.co.uk/online-marketing_1) offers valuable insight into social media and the power of search engine optimisation. It also explores the use of business blogs and mobile apps as other ways to improve your company's public status on the web.
>
> Also, the ability to sell and get the best out of the selling process is among the most important skills any entrepreneur has to have. You can also find out all about this area at Startups (www.startups.co.uk/the-sales-process).

Establishing a marketing budget

Once you are in business, putting together a cost budget is a whole lot easier. With a baseline to work from and some experience of how effective past expenditure was you can make some realistic projections. For your first budget that's a whole lot harder, but you need the figures for your cashflow.

Start by listing your expenditure plans under the categories outlined in Tables 7.1 and 7.2. Then work out how much you will need to spend in each area to achieve your goal. So, for example, if producing a catalogue and mailing it to 5,000 potential customers is one of your marketing expenses, include those costs in your marketing budget.

> ### Startups Tip
> One rough and ready check on your marketing budget is to state the overall figure as a percentage of sales. So if your sales objective is £100,000 a 10% marketing budget would call for a figure of £10,000. You can get a feel for the amount being spent on marketing by looking at the published accounts of competing businesses.

You don't have to be a rocket scientist to come up with a good business marketing strategy, and it needn't cost that much either. Startups (www.startups.co.uk/low-cost-marketing-strategy.html) provides a range of valuable ideas from building mailing lists to creating a press release.

Checklist

☑ Analyse what type of advertising and promotion others in your industry use to reach their markets.

☑ Describe your product/service range: what is your main selling message that will hook in your customers?

☑ Work out your marketing expense to sales ratio and analyse why you have settled on that figure.

☑ Set down the activity conversion rates for your main marketing activities.

☑ Consider how you will know if you are getting good value for your marketing spend.

↻ CHAPTER 8
Operations

📖 What's in this chapter?

Aside from staff, the big cost areas in your business plan
will be concerned with getting your product or service
into shape to be bought. These expenses will include a
range of very different items, from finding premises and
getting equipped, through to sourcing supplies. Not all
of these areas will apply to every type of business nor
will the costs necessarily be incurred at the outset. For
example many start-up ventures launch from home and
those involved in expansion strategies often put a toe in
the water first using serviced premises. Your business
plan should show your thinking behind each area as well
as a realistic estimate of their financial implications.

In this chapter we'll cover:

→ *assembling your product*
→ *using outsourcing*
→ *deciding on premises*

→ getting equipped
→ finding suppliers
→ building your website
→ working from home.

Assembling your product

Businesses are fundamentally involved in adding value to bought-in resources. For Not In The High Street this means putting together a great website to help other people sell their goods. Yo! Sushi adds value by selling bought-in ingredients through well-sited outlets. For Hotel Chocolat, value is added by a continuous stream of product innovations that its customers have a hand in developing. These are then marketed online and through a chain of retail outlets located in key urban areas sited so as to maximise brand visibility. Your business plan needs to show what 'ingredients' you will be assembling, and later how you will add value to them.

Prototype problems

If your product or service is not ready for sale, for example it may need more design work, testing or customer feedback, that should be built into your business plan. A table similar to Table 8.1 should be completed and included in your business plan. The example in the table is for a hypothetical new product, Father's Day chocolate treat. The prototype development plan shows that we need nine weeks to have a product ready for sale; we expect to require £17,000 to

TABLE 8.1: Example prototype development plan

Product/ service	State of develop- ment	Tasks to be carried out	Comple- tion date	Costs	Mile- stones
Father's Day chocolate treat	Recipe written	1. Customer acceptance trials	1. Eight weeks	1. £5,000	1.a) Samples prepared – week 4
		2. Packaging to be designed	2. Nine weeks	2. £10,000	1.b) Run tasting sessions – week 6
		3. Promotion copy to be written	3. Nine weeks	3. £2,000	1.c) Review findings – week 7
Totals			Nine weeks	£17,000	

fund the three main elements of work involved. For task 1, customer acceptance, there are three subtasks: preparing the samples, running tasting sessions and reviewing the findings from those. These three subtasks are in effect milestones on the way to achieving our goal of getting a new product ready to sell. An outside backer would expect to see such milestones included in your business plan so they can be reassured that their cash is being used effectively.

Planning production

Production here is used in the broadest sense. Your business plan has to show what processes will be used to turn your raw materials into finished goods. Issues to consider include the following.

→ If you are making a physical product, describe the process used to get from the raw materials to the finished goods.

→ List any machinery, tools and equipment required, along with their output limits, cost and date required (see Table 8.2).

→ Describe any quality standards that you have to adhere to – hygiene, safety etc. This is particularly important for businesses involved with catering, food, health and electrical goods, gas or any product that might pose a risk to users. This may also extend to labelling, where legislation on product descriptions, weights and measures applies.

Table 8.2: Example production equipment plan

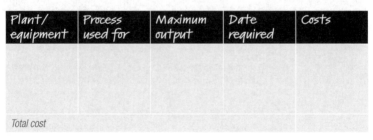

Plant/ equipment	Process used for	Maximum output	Date required	Costs
Total cost				

> **Startups Tip**
> You don't have to buy new equipment from the outset. Investors will look favourably on a business plan that incorporates sensible economies. Aside from eBay, these are two useful sites where you can search for second-hand business equipment: Greasy Machines (www. greasymachines.com) and MM Börse Online (www.mm-boerse.de).

Using outsourcing

Outsourcing, contracting out the whole or part of your business operations, is a popular strategy. There is almost no area of business that can't be carried out on your behalf by someone else. Agents can sell for you, subcontractors can produce, fulfilment companies can hold stock and deliver on your behalf.

Co-founder of smoothie company innocent drinks, Richard Reed, has these thoughts on outsourcing: "Whether you partner up or whether you do it yourself is a big decision, and for us what we've learnt is: work out what you're good at, and work out where the real value is, and really do those things yourself. So at innocent, we buy all the fruits ourselves, and we develop all the fruits ourselves, and all the recipes ourselves. So I can guarantee anything that is in an innocent bottle is unique to innocent and is always the best quality. What we haven't done is own the manufacturing sites, because that costs millions of pounds to build a factory. It's not the factory that makes the fruit better quality, it's the fruit in the first place. We don't do anything to the fruit – it just goes down through the crushers into the bottles. So we've benefitted hugely from owning the bit where the value's created, but outsourcing the bit where the capital is tied up, but doesn't add much value to the whole project."

> **Startups Tip**
> Outsourcing reduces the amount of investment that your business plan has to support. This means you may have to raise less money initially, and that may in turn be easier to secure.

Some things are central to your business and you should not outsource them, at least at the outset until you have them fully under control. These include cashflow management and most aspects of customer relations. Later on you may consider, for example, outsourcing collecting cash from customers to an invoice discounter or factoring service, which may have better processes in place to handle larger volumes of invoices than you can afford.

One way to set the boundaries for outsourcing is to decide what you are good at then outsource everything else. In other words, focus your company on your core competency, and 'stick to the knitting'. That logic is sound in theory, and to a certain degree in practice, but like everything else you can take it too far. The key is to understand your business and its goals and decide how outsourcing can help you attain them.

In my experience

Nick Jenkins, Moonpig

"Immediately after registering the company I hired a website design agency to help build and design the site. Inconsistent service from this agency made me decide to bring the whole IT function in-house, hiring a software developer to build a completely new site."

Deciding on premises

There are a number of factors to bear in mind when choosing where to operate, the most costly of which is whether to rent or buy. Buying a premises gives you all sorts of advantages, not least that you can make any alterations you want (if the law allows) without going cap in hand to a landlord, and of course no one can kick you out. On the downside, you have to invest a substantial amount of money up front and you have to sell up if you outgrow the premises. You of course enjoy any rise in the value of the property, but have to be prepared for markets to fall or, worse still, freeze up altogether.

Renting is not without its problems, however. You have to take on the property for a number of years, and even if you sublet with the landlord's permission, you are liable for rent for the full period should the person you sublet to default. Rents are reviewed, almost invariably upwards, every three to seven years. You are expected to keep the property in good repair and return it to the landlord at the end of the lease period in the condition it was at the outset. That can prove expensive if the landlord doesn't share your opinion that any changes you have made constitute an improvement.

Decide how much space is needed, making a prudent balance between having room for modest expansion with carrying too big a cost burden from the outset.

Check out how near your customers you have to be.

Ensure that if you need skilled or specialist labour, it is readily available.

Make certain any necessary back-up services are available.

Research the local availability of essential raw materials, components and other supplies.

Investigate the cost of premises, rates and utilities and compare with other areas.

Explore how accessible the site is by road, rail, air and other public transport.

Investigate if there are any changes in the pipeline that might adversely affect trade, eg a new motorway bypassing the town, changes in transport services, closure of a large factory.

Make enquiries to establish if there are competing businesses in the immediate neighbourhood and determine whether these will have a beneficial or detrimental effect.

Determine if the location is conducive to the creation of a favourable market image. For instance, a luxury food producer may lack credibility trading from an area notorious for its dirt and pollution.

Establish if the area is generally regarded as low or high growth.

Make enquiries to ensure that the area is pro business.

Look into whether you and your key employees can get to the area easily and quickly without undue cost.

> **Startups Tip**
>
> Use Trimble's free program, Sketchup (http://sketchup.google.com), a 3D modelling software tool to work out how much space you will need to operate in. Alternatively, for around £90, you can buy a package from Smart Draw (www.smartdraw.com/specials/officeplanning.asp); you can try it for free before you buy.

Getting equipped

Once you have found the right premises and put in any manufacturing machinery, your business plan should show what other equipment you will need. A number of items such as furniture, shelving, filing, telephone and computing equipment are common to many types of business. Some require more specialised items. High-end printers, specialist software, electronic point of sale (EPOS) tills, bar coders, stereo systems for background music, lighting, satellite navigation systems and video projectors are some of the specialist equipment that certain types of venture may have to build into their business plan expenses.

Use Table 8.3 on the opposite page to get your equipment costs into shape ready to enter into your business plan. In Chapters 10 and 11 I will explain how to use this information.

TABLE 8.3: Equipment cost plan

	Item(s)	Supplier	Date Required	Costs
Specialist Equipment				
General Business Equipment: Phones, PCs, Software, ISP, Photocopier etc				
Office Fittings: Desks, Chairs, Shelving, Filing Cabinets etc				
Security: Alarms, Shutters, First Aid, Fire Extinguishers etc				
Signs and Notices: External, Internal, Health and Safety, Fire Exits etc				
Staff Facilities: Kettle, Microwave				
Vehicles: Cars, Vans etc				
Other Equipment				
Total Cost				

Startups Tip

Alliance & Leicester (now part of Santander) has a useful business equipment cost calculator (www.allianceleicestercommercialbank.co.uk/bizguides/full/costcalc/index.asp) showing cost categories and approximate values for a wide variety of different business from acupuncture practices through to windscreen services, taking in convenience stores, furniture makers and used car dealerships on the way.

Finding suppliers

The terms of trade you negotiate will have a significant effect on your cashflow projections, so choose your suppliers carefully. Business-to-business directories such as Kelly Search (www.kellysearch.co.uk), Kompass (www.kompass.co.uk) and Applegate (www.applegate.co.uk)

between them have global databases of over 2.4 million industrial and commercial companies in 190 countries, listing over 230,000 product categories. You can search by category, country and brand name.

The areas that you should note in your business plan are:

-▷ terms of trade, payment and credit given

-▷ level of service

-▷ who else they supply, getting feedback from their customers

-▷ guarantees and warranties offered

-▷ price comparisons demonstrating that they are competitive.

Other buying options

Aside from searching out suppliers through directories and word of mouth, consider one or more of the following strategies.

Bartering online

You can save using up your cash by bartering your products and services for those of other businesses. Organisations that can help you get started with bartering include Bartercard (www.bartercard.co.uk) and Barter Marketing (www.bartermarketing.com).

Buying online

There are over 200 price comparison websites covering computer hardware and software, phones, travel, credit cards, bank accounts, loans, utilities, electrical goods, office products including inkjet and printer supplies and a few thousand more items a business might purchase. Paler.com, a quirky website run by Petru Palre (www.paler.com), has a directory listing these sites, with brief explanations and helpful comment page where users have inserted more sites and additional information.

> **Startups Tip**
>
> No business is an island. You need to buy products and services from other companies and organisations in order for your business to operate. The section in Startups on this topic (www.startups.co.uk/product-suppliers) covers everything from negotiating good deals on stock, to how to set up favourable credit agreements and deal with late payments.

Building your website

While it is possible to piggyback on other businesses' websites – eBay and Amazon, for example – most business will need to cost in their own for their business plan. A website can be used for a variety of important strategic purposes aside from selling. You can use it to get paid, recruit staff, deliver additional services, communicate with your customers, run market research surveys, host online communities and generate advertising revenue.

To get some idea of what to include and exclude from your website, check out your competitors' websites and those of any other business that you rate highly. You can also get some pointers from the Web Marketing Association's Web Awards (www.webaward.org). There you can see the best websites in each business sector. Also check out The Good Web Guide (www.thegoodwebguide.co.uk), which contains thousands of detailed website reviews.

Once you have decided on your website you will be able to build those costs into your business plan. You have two main options here, with very different cost implications.

Doing it yourself

You probably already have a basic website writing tool as part of your office software. If you use Microsoft, visit Microsoft Office Live (www.office.microsoft.com) for links to free web design tools. Also, you will find literally hundreds of packages from £50 to around £500, which with varying amounts of support will help you create your own website. Web Wiz Guide (www.webwizguide.com) has a tutorial covering the basics of web page design and layout.

> ### Startups Tip
> Top Ten Reviews (www.toptenreviews.com) provides an annual report on the best website creation software rated by ease of use, help and support, value for money and a score of other factors.
>
> Startups (www.startups.co.uk/managing-your-website) can show you how to manage your website effectively and keep it updated. Here you will find pointers on everything from online security to increasing traffic to your site, as well as valuable insight into search engine optimisation.

Getting outside help

There are literally thousands of consultants claiming to be able to create a website. Prices start from £499 where an off-the-peg website package will be tweaked slightly to meet your needs, to around £5,000 to get something closer to a site tailormade for you. The Directory of Design Consultants (www.designdirectory.co.uk) and Web Design Directory (www.web-design-directory-uk.co.uk) list hundreds of consultants, some single-person companies and others somewhat larger. You can look at their websites to see whether you will like what they do. Web Design Directory has some useful pointers on choosing a designer.

> ### Startups Tip
> To keep costs to a minimum, consider auctioning off your web design project. With sites such as Freelancer (www.freelancer.com) you state how much you are prepared to pay with a description of the project and freelancers around the world bid under your price, with the lowest bidder winning.

Other website costs to plan for

As well as your website you will need to budget for a number of ongoing costs in your business plan.

⤏ ISP to keep you online – upwards of £100 per annum.

⤏ Registering your domain name – £80 plus, for two years.

⤏ Search engine optimisation, such as that provided by Submit Express (www.submitexpress.xo.uk), Rank4u (www.rank4u.co.uk) and Wordtracker (www.wordtracker.com). These services aim to move you into the all-important top 10 ranking in key search engines. Payment methods vary, for example Rank4u have a No Placement, No Fee deal where it only gets paid once it has achieved the positioning you want. 123 Ranking (www.123ranking.co.uk) has optimisation packages aimed at small and new businesses from £199 per annum.

⤏ Paid inclusion and placement may be necessary if you don't want to wait for search engines to find your website. The only way to be sure you appear early on the first page or two of a search is to advertise in a paid placement listing. For major search engines such as Google AdWords (www.google.com), Yahoo Search Marketing (http://searchmarketing.yahoo.com) and Microsoft adCenter (https:adcenter.Microsoft.com), you will be invited to bid on the terms you want to appear for, by way of a set sum per click.

⤏ Website updates will be essential as static or rarely updated websites don't attract or retain much traffic.

💡 JARGON BUSTER

Gadgets (or widgets) are small programmes such as weather forecasts, currency convertors, calorie counters, jokes, life tips, calculators or translators. They are a low-cost way to keep your website fresh. Google (www.google.com/ig/directory) at the last count supplied over 200,000 free gadgets.

Working from home

Starting out in business from home has a number of important cost benefits that may make any business plan a more interesting proposition. Aside from lower costs, you will generally be able to start up quicker, cut down on travelling time and cut out a stressful commute. Bankers tend to favour business plans for home-based operations as the risks are lower at the all-important start-up stage. Venture capital providers may see this as a sign of thinking too small and be less enthusiastic.

Your business plan should confirm that you have:

⇥ checked that you are legally allowed to run this type of business from your home

⇥ sufficient space to operate effectively

⇥ approval from your mortgagor and or any co-owner in writing

⇥ informed your insurance company

⇥ planning consent and business regulation approval for any alterations to be made

⇥ checked the position with regard to business rates.

> ✐ **Startups Tip**
> For more information on all aspects of working from home, visit Startups (www.startups.co.uk/working-from-home).

Checklist

☑ Consider what activities, if any, you could outsource.

☑ Identify what type and size of premises you will need.

☑ Ascertain the terms of trade of any suppliers.

☑ Consider how you intend to set up, operate and keep your website up to date.

↻ CHAPTER 9

Management – staffing – you

📖 What's in this chapter?

Business is more about people than product.
Nothing gets achieved without someone somewhere
doing something, and doing it right. Whether working
on your own, with partners or employing staff, your
business plan should show how you are going to ensure
the results you are aiming for are going to be achieved
by those involved. What's more, if your plan is intended
to help raise finance, your reader will expect you to
either have built or be building a team. They know that
a business with some depth in terms of staffing is more
secure; illness or peak periods can be better handled. It
will also give the business some headroom for growth,
an essential feature for any venture capital provision.

In this chapter we'll cover:

→ *your business skills and experience*
→ *identifying the founders' and partners' roles
   within the business*

→ building a team: assessing what people you'll need and when

→ forging an external team

→ using a balanced scorecard.

Your business skills and experience

Neither super-intelligence nor an MBA are essential to plan a business. Many successful entrepreneurs didn't go to university, or even spend that much time at school. Sir Richard Branson (Virgin) dropped out of full-time education at 16. Lord Sugar (Amstrad), Sir Philip Green (BHS and Arcadia, Sir Bernie Ecclestone (Formula One) and Charles Dunstone (Carphone Warehouse) all bypassed university education. Some who went to university didn't stay there long. Steve Jobs (Apple) and Bill Gates (Microsoft) left after a semester or two. But don't worry too much if you do have a university degree; education is no bar to planning a successful venture. Stelios Haji-Iannou, founder of easyJet, has a BSc from the London School of Economics and an MSc from Cass Business School at City University, London; Google's founders, Sergey Brin and Larry Page, both graduated from Stanford.

Your business plan should have enough information about you to demonstrate the following.

→ You have taken the initiative and made things happen somewhere before, ideally in a business environment. If you have started up, grown or held a management position in any other business here is the place to shout about it. Use tangible facts where possible, such as "I was responsible for launching xyz product into the UK market, generating sales and profits of zyx and yzx market share", supported with evidence – ideal material for an appendix.

→ You have some direct and relevant experience of the product/ market area. Simon Nixon, co-founder of Money Supermarket, knew very little about the software programs that were crucial to the launch of the venture. Despite some fairly complicated technology, the business model he was using involved little more than the tried and tested role of the intermediary or broker doing the sums for their client that he used when he started his first business.

→ You understand enough about finance to tell the difference between cash and profit; know the difference between debt and equity; appreciate the importance of timely and accurate accounts; and understand how to calculate your break-even sales level. Although Simon Nixon dropped out from an accounting course at Nottingham University (leaving halfway through the second year), he had sufficient grasp of finance to get a £1 billion business floated on the London Stock Market. If you don't feel comfortable in this area now, by the time you have worked through Chapter 10 you will.

→ You have the capacity to see things through even when the going gets tough. If you don't have an example from your business experience, use one from another aspect of your life. Sailing, diving, skiing, mountaineering and hiking are all areas rich in opportunities to show that you can stick at a task through thick and thin.

→ You have learned from areas you may have failed in or from made mistakes in the past. Rising from the ashes of former disasters is a common feature of many successful entrepreneurs. Henry Ford had been bankrupted twice before, in his 40th year, founding the Ford Motor Corporation with a loan of $28,000. Milton Hershey started three unsuccessful candy companies in Philadelphia, Chicago and New York before starting Hershey's, which brought milk chocolate (previously a Swiss delicacy) to the masses. Walt Disney's first business, Laugh-O-Gram, was so unsuccessful that at one point he resorted to eating dog food to stay alive.

> **Startups Tip**
> You shouldn't boast about your expertise or achievements, but if you have accomplished something important and noteworthy this is the time to bring it to the fore.

Identifying the founders' and partners' roles within the business

Many of the most successful business ventures involve two or more people working in partnership. The reason that this is such a successful model seems to be that the business can draw on a broader range of skills, and that financiers prefer backing teams rather than loners. Examples of businesses with more than one founder at the helm, at least at one point in their development, include Ben Cohen and Jerry Greenfield (Ben and Jerry's Ice Cream), Bill Gates and Paul Allen (Microsoft), Steve Jobs and Steve Wozniak (Apple), Sergey Brin and Larry Page (Google) and Mark Zuckerberg, Dustin Moskovitz and Chris Hughes (Facebook). Nixon persuaded Duncan Cameron, a computer geek who was his girlfriend's brother, to give up a computer studies course at Liverpool University to write software programs that were crucial to the launch of Money Supermarket.

If you are planning a team start-up, bear in mind your partners' skills and attributes when you are assessing your own abilities. For example, Michael Marks was a great market stall operator, but it was Thomas Spencer's organisational and bookkeeping skills, and his contacts with manufacturers, which allowed the business to really flourish. He also brought £300 by way of investment to the Marks & Spencer business, for which he made a more than adequate return.

The legal aspects of forming a partnership are covered in Chapter 12, as those have a bearing on the capital structure of a venture. But the relationship, skills and the roles of yourself and your partner(s) are if anything more important. You should show the role, relevant experience, resources that your partners will bring to the venture over the period covered by the business plan together with their share of the ownership. Filling in a grid such as that shown in Table 9.1 will help you do this more easily.

Table 9.1: Roles, experience, resources and ownership

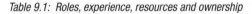

Who	Role in business	Relevant experience	Financial or other resources brought in	Share of owner-ship
Founder				
Partner 1				
Partner 2				

In my experience

Sophie Cornish and Holly Tucker, Notonthehighstreet.com

"We had both run our own businesses before joining forces on Notonthehighstreet.com. We met a decade earlier, while working for an advertising agency, and went on to set up ventures in the events and shopping sectors. With very different working backgrounds and experience we complement each other well. One of us (Holly) has a background in sales, while the other (Sophie) has experience in building brands. We have a great working relationship, though we do disagree – productively – from time to time. From the outset we had the same vision, and are totally focused on the same goal."

Building a team: assessing what people you'll need and when

> **Startups Tip**
>
> Taking on employees is a massive step. It's also a legal minefield, not to mention a massive financial burden to recruit members of staff. Visit the Startups section on this topic (www.startups.co.uk/small-business-hiring), which covers everything you need to be aware of, from writing a job advert to the interview and staff induction process.

Aside from your partner(s), if your venture will require additional staffing over the period of the business plan you should answer the following questions, using a grid as shown in Table 9.2.

⇢ What role they will have in the business?

⇢ What key performance indicators (KPIs) will you use to ensure that they are doing a good job? For sales people this could be turnover, new accounts opened, sales growth achieved. For a staff job, such as accounts, the measure could be producing the figures accurately and by a prescribed date each month.

JARGON BUSTER

Key Performance Indicators, also known as KPIs, show how an organisation defines and measures the steps on the road to achieving important objectives such as sales, profit or market share.

TABLE 9.2: Staffing plan

Job title	Role in business	KPIs	When required	Pay	How they will be recruited	Who will manage them	Likely team role

⇨ How much will you pay them and how does that compare to the going rate?

⇨ Who will manage, motivate and lead the area in which the people concerned will be working?

⇨ How will you search for and recruit new staff?

⇨ What attributes beyond the specific skills for the job will you be looking for?

⇨ What particular strengths will new employees bring to your team and how will those keep your organisation well balanced?

Paying staff what they deserve can be a thorny issue. Founder of pharmaceutical company Waymade Healthcare, Vijay Patel, has this to say on the subject: "Most entrepreneurs don't overspend on themselves. I fall into that category. All the revenue besides comfortable living goes back to develop the business. All the profits are ploughed back for the next stage of your evolution. No yachts, no private planes, just what you see here. Another thing that entrepreneurs do not recognise is that people who have their careers with you have the same aspirations for their careers and families as you have. So you make sure you pay them well, you grow their CVs by stretching them, and you encourage their continuous development. That's the only way they're going to stay with you."

Recruiting staff is only half the battle. In fact, that's where it really starts to get complicated. Startups (www.startups.co.uk/hr-and-management) will walk you through everything you need to know about managing your team, and fostering a healthy and productive working environment for your staff and ultimately your business.

> ### Startups Tip
> The easiest ways to find the going rate for a new employee is to look at advertisements for similar jobs in your area or visit PayScale (www.payscale.com), where you can get accurate real-time information on pay scales.

People are different, and team members must not only have 'technical' skills such as being an accountant or sales person, but must also have a valuable team role. Experts in team behaviour have identified the key team profiles that are essential if it is to function well. Being creative, analytical, dependable, outgoing, introverted, challenging or compliant are personal attributes which play a part in making for a successful team. Too much of one attribute (or its deficiency) can make a team lopsided and so function poorly, or worse.

Dr Meredith Belbin and his research team at Henley Management College observed that successful teams were made up of individuals displaying one or more of nine different team roles to varying degrees. Belbin's website (www.belbin.com) provides both the theory behind teams and practical ways to build a great team.

Teams can deliver superior motivation, enhanced co-ordination, improved problem solving and better decision making. But that comes at a price: decisions can be slow to make; training may be required; and teams take time to bed in and require lots of patience.

Forging an external team

Not everyone vital to your business plan will be on your payroll. Nonetheless, they will be important in building credibility for your business.

Strategic alliances

The most successful businesses forge relationships with businesses up and down their supply chain that go beyond simply buying and selling. Starbucks has an alliance with Yahoo and Apple to offer digital content to customers. Their aim is to counter the competition from McDonald's, which only started selling freshly ground coffee in 2007, but now sell more coffee in the UK than Costa and Starbucks combined. Strada creator and Côte founder, Andy Bassadone, offers this warning on supply chain relationships: "The temptation is to always go for the cheapest – the cheapest is not always the solution. It's better you have a good long-term relationship with your suppliers, especially in the food business, than necessarily always competing with other suppliers to keep the prices low. Obviously, there's got to be an element of that but ultimately it is a sort of partnership".

In my experience

Mary and Doug Perkins, Specsavers

"Partnership is at the heart of our success, and no matter what market we are in, it is the partnerships with the professionals that allows our business to grow."

Professional advisors

There is a tendency towards secrecy amongst those writing business plans. However, with the right protection in place (see Chapter 16 for information on non-disclosure agreements), there is no reason not to take outside advice, and indeed every reason to do so. Anyone reading your business plan will draw comfort from the fact that they are not the first, and that your ideas have been honed on the wisdom and experience of others. In fact, the more qualified, experienced and prestigious your advisors, the more their input will enhance your business plan, in the eyes of the reader. After all, rather than being the untested ideas of one or two people, they have been validated by professionals. You will add real value to your proposition by getting an accountant to look over the figures, a lawyer the IP rights, an engineer your prototype design and a software consultant your website plans.

Using a balanced scorecard

This may sound like a piece of business jargon (which of course strictly speaking it is), but the balanced scorecard is a powerful and efficient way of demonstrating the thinking behind your organisation and how the team you have in mind will help deliver the results your business plan describes (see Figure 9.1). Everything you can do to demonstrate to your readers (and yourself!) the reasoning behind what may well be your biggest single long-term cost – wages – the stronger your proposal will be.

> ### JARGON BUSTER
>
> The balanced scorecard is a management process that sets out to align business activities to the vision and strategy of the organisation, improve internal and external communications, and monitor an organisation's performance against strategic goals. It adds non-financial performance measures to traditional financial targets to give managers and directors a more 'balanced' view of organisational performance.

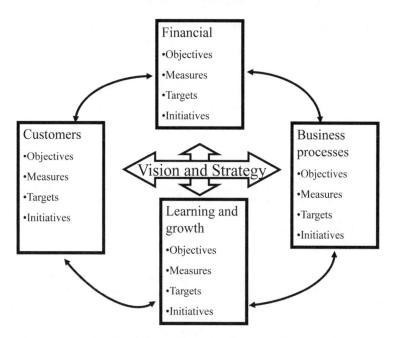

Figure 9.1 Using the balanced scorecard in your business plan

Four perspectives are included in the business plan process and a number of objectives, measures, targets and initiatives can be set to achieve specific KPIs for each perspective.

1. **Financial:** these include KPIs for return on investment, cashflow, profit margins and shareholder value.

2. **Customer:** here the KPIs can be for customer retention rates, satisfaction levels, referrals and complaints.

3. **Internal business processes:** these can include stock turn, accident rates, defects in production, reduction in the number of processes and improvements in communications.

4. **Learning and growth:** employee turnover, morale levels, training and development achievements and internal promotions versus new recruits are all KPIs to use here.

The four perspectives are linked by a double feedback loop whose purpose is to ensure that KPIs are not in conflict with one another. For example, if customer satisfaction could be achieved by improving delivery times, achieving that by, say, increasing stock levels might conflict with a financial target of improving return on capital employed (see Chapter 10 for a refresher on financial ratios).

 Checklist

☑ List your skills, knowledge and experience relevant to this business. Do the same for any partners and complete a grid such as shown in Table 9.1.

☑ If you are taking on a partner, identify in what way their skills complement yours and why you are sure you will work well together.

☑ Consider which external advisors you could tap into.

☑ Consider whether you could/should form any strategic alliances.

☑ Using Figure 9.1, set out the KPIs that can be used to track achievement against your business plan.

↪ *CHAPTER 10*
Preparing financial reports

📖 What's in this chapter?

Finance is certainly not an exact science. Even the most enthusiastic accountant would not make that claim. Nevertheless, anyone reading your business plan will pay great attention to the numbers, and, crucially, to the thinking behind those numbers. Much of that thinking – about product, marketing strategy, how you will operate, the staffing levels required – has been covered in previous chapters.

In this chapter we'll cover:

→ *making sales projections*
→ *forecasting cashflow*
→ *setting out the profit and loss account*
→ *building a balance sheet*
→ *estimating your break-even point*
→ *using ratios*
→ *keeping the books*
→ *pulling it all together.*

Making sales projections

All your financial numbers are derived in one way or another from the projections you make for sales. The more you sell, the more bought-in goods and services you will require, the more stock you will carry, credit customer financing will be higher, and paperwork and administration volumes will all increase. The converse is true, also.

Your first sales forecast

> **Startups Tip**
>
> Don't forget to build seasonal factors into your forecasts. For example, in the summer months you would expect sales of certain products, swimwear, ice creams and suntan lotion, for example, to be higher than, say, in the winter. Ski equipment would probably follow a reverse pattern.

If you haven't started out in business yet, or if the business plan you are writing involves new products or markets, then you have no history to go on; this is always a tough call. Your business plan should have the following areas covered to substantiate your first forecast.

⇨ **Customers in the pipeline:** how many customers and potential customers do you know who are likely to buy from you, and how much might they buy? Here you can use many types of data on which to base reasonable sales projections. You can interview a sample of prospective customers, issue a press release or advertisement to gauge response, and exhibit at trade shows to obtain customer reactions.

⇨ **Market share:** how big is the market for your product or service and what is the competitive position? These factors were examined in Chapter 5, and can provide a market share basis for your forecasts. An entry market share of more than a few per cent is most unusual. But beware of turning this argument on its head. Unsubstantiated statements such as 'In a market of £1 billion per annum we can easily capture 1%, which is £1 million a year' will not impress any investor.

⟶ **How others have fared:** you can gather some useful knowledge on similar businesses by researching company records at Companies House (www.companieshouse.gov.uk), where the accounts of most British companies are kept, or by talking with the founders of similar ventures who aren't your direct competitors.

> ### Startups Tip
> Your sales projections have to be believable. Most lenders and investors have extensive experience of similar business proposals. Unlike you, they have the benefit of hindsight, being able to look back several years at other ventures they have backed, and see how they fared in practice as compared with their initial forecasts.

Base sales forecasts after year one

Whilst your business plan will contain your sales objectives, that is, what you want to achieve over the coming three years or so, the base forecast is the most likely future outcome given what has happened in the past. That forecast provides the momentum to underpin the sales figures that you put into your cashflow and profit projections. Figure 10.1 over the page shows an example sales history for years one to three; the trend of those sales over the coming three years; and the sales objectives for the next three years that will be used for the financials of the business plan. You can see that the objectives are moving well ahead of trend, and it is filling this gap that your marketing strategy needs to justify.

Fitting a trend line to historic data is done by extending a line through the data that best fits that data. The easy way is to use graph paper and fit the line by eye. There is a mathematical technique – linear regression – that will do this for you. For business planning purposes this is probably overkill, but using it may well impress your reader!

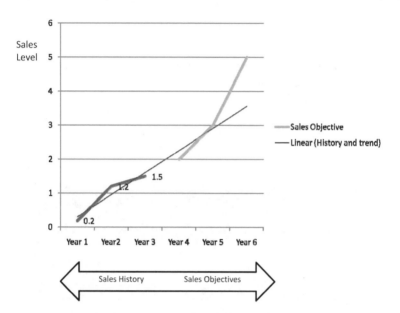

Figure 10.1 Sales history, trend and future objectives

> **Startups Tip**
>
> Microsoft's Charts tool allows you to insert a trend line on your data. Right clicking on the relevant line in your chart will give you five trend line options.

Forecasting tools

With a sales history, there are a number of techniques that can make forecasting easier and more credible to your readers.

→ **Moving average:** this method takes a series of data from the past, say, the last six months' sales, adds them up, divides by the number of months and uses that figure as being the most likely forecast of what will happen in month seven. This method works well in a static, mature marketplace where change happens slowly, if at all.

⇢ **Weighted moving average:** this method gives the most recent data more significance than earlier data since the former is a better representation of current business conditions. So before adding up the series of data, each figure is weighted by multiplying it by an increasingly higher factor as you get closer to the most recent data.

There are a number of much more sophisticated forecasting techniques, but for business planning purposes the ones discussed in this chapter will be sufficient to show you have applied some serious thought to your sales projections.

Forecasting cashflow

Cashflow is perhaps the single most important financial element of any business plan. It's here that the funding requirements of the business are set out and when you expect to be in positive territory.

The layout of a cashflow forecast is set out in Table 10.1 on the next page. In the example, cash sales is the only source of cash in the first month; however, sales were made to business customers who are expected to pay up in the following month. So from the second month onwards there are two sources of cash. The figures for sales receipts come from your sales forecast (see above).

Payments are made over all three months for ongoing expenses, wages, salaries, utilities and the like. Equipment features only in the first two months. The bottom two rows of the cashflow forecast show the net cash surplus/deficit of the month, with the cumulative cash surplus/deficit shown below. The figures for your payments come from your operating (see Chapter 8) and staffing plans (see Chapter 9).

The cumulative cash surplus/deficit row shows how much cash the business needs to deliver the level of sales set out in the business plan.

TABLE 10.1: Cashflow forecast example

	Month	April A	May B	June C
	Sales receipts			
	Cash sales	10,000	15,000	20,000
	Credit sales		10,000	12,000
1	Total cash in	10,000	25,000	32,000
	Payments			
	Salary and wages	1,000	1,200	1,500
	Utilities	500	500	500
	Rent and rates	500	500	500
	Materials	5,000	5,000	10,000
	Equipment	25,000	11,000	
2	Total cash out	32,000	18,200	12,500
3	Monthly cash surplus/ deficit [1–2]	(22,000)	6,800	19,500
4	Cumulative cash surplus/deficit	(22,000)	(15,200) [3B–4A]	4,300 [3C–4B]

> **Startups Tip**
> Using a spreadsheet saves time, will reduce arithmetic errors and let you try out a number of 'what ifs', such as lower or higher levels of sales and expenses, with differing build up speeds.

Your business plan should project cashflow month by month for the first year and then quarterly until you are showing a cash surplus (Table 10.2).

> **Startups Tip**
> There is a useful cashflow tool on the Startups website (www. startups.co.uk/cashflow-calculator.html).

TABLE 10.2: Business plan cashflow template

	Year 1												Year 2			
Month/ quarter	1	2	3	4	5	6	7	8	9	10	11	12	1	2	3	4
Receipts																
Cash sales																
Credit sales																
Total cash in																
Payments																
Salary and wages																
Utilities																
Rent and rates																
Marketing																
Equipment																
Total cash out																
Monthly cash surplus/ deficit																
Cumulative cash surplus/ deficit																

Setting out the profit and loss account

Cashflow keeps a business alive, paying the bills as they occur and getting money in from customers, but profit is what tells you if it's worth launching into business or expanding. Table 10.3 on the next page presents an example profit and loss account (based loosely on the figures in Table 10.1).

The sales turnover comprises the cash sales (45,000), the credit sales for which cash has already come in (22,000) and 12,000 of credit sales made in the last month, which will not show up in cashflow until the following month. The cashflow shows 20,000 has been paid out for materials, but we can assume that not all of that has been used up, and 5,000 is left in stock for use at a later date.

TABLE 10.3: Example profit and loss account

Profit and loss account for year ended 20XX	
Sales turnover	79,000
Less cost of sales (materials used)	15,000
Gross profit	**64,000**
Less operating costs	
Salary and wages	3,700
Utilities	1,500
Rent and rates	1,500
Total operating costs	6,700
Operating profit	**57,300**
Less	
Interest on borrowings	1,000
Depreciation	12,000
Profit before tax	44,300
Tax at 20%	8,860
Net profit after tax	**35,440**

Deducting the materials used from the sales turnover gives us the gross profit, another key number in the business plan, the significance of which will be covered later in this chapter. You can see the term 'cost of sales' used here as in practice there may be costs other than materials such as production wages, energy costs used in manufacturing machinery etc.

Next, costs such as general salaries, rent, rates, utilities, marketing expenditure and insurance are deducted to arrive at the operating profit. Finally, the costs associated with financing the business such as interest, are deducted, as is tax. You will notice on the cashflow, 36,000 was paid out for equipment. Unlike wages, utilities, materials and so forth, equipment is not paid for generally as it is used. The way this is treated in the accounts is to write off the cost by way of depreciation over the working life of the asset. In this case we have assumed the 36,000 will last for three accounting periods, so 12,000 is taken into the profit and loss account by way of depreciation expense for each period.

TABLE 10.4: Summarised three-year profit and loss account

Period	Year 1	Year 2	Year 3
Sales turnover			
Less cost of sales			
Gross profit			
Less operating costs			
Operating profit			
Less			
Interest on borrowings			
Depreciation			
Profit before tax			
Tax at			
Net profit after tax			

Net profit after tax, generally known as the 'bottom line', is the profit left for the owners/shareholders either to take out or reinvest.

Your business plan should contain a summarised profit and loss account in the body of the plan, covering a period of at least three years (see Table 10.4 above). A more detailed account should be included in an appendix.

> **Startups Tip**
> Whilst cashflow measures the amount of cash in and out of a business, profit (or loss) is a measure of economic activity. Look at Table 10.1. For April, the cash from sales was 10,000, but the sales turnover was probably nearer 20,000, as the 10,000 of credit sales being paid for in May was most likely generated in the preceding month.

Building a balance sheet

The third accounting document that should be included in your business plan is the balance sheet (Table 10.5 over the page). Reported by venture capitalists and banks as the most often missed element of a

TABLE 10.5: Example balance sheet

Balance sheet at 31 March 20XX				
Tangible long-term assets with life over one year	*Fixed assets*	*36,000*		
	Less depreciation	*12,000*		
	Net book value			**24,000**
Working capital, assets (CA) and liabilities (CL) expected to be due or realised within a year	*Current assets (CA)*			
	Stock	*5,000*		
	Debtors	*12,000*		
	Cash	*4,300*		
	Total current assets		**21,300**	
	Less current liabilities (CL)			
	Overdraft	*0*		
	Creditors	*5,000*		
	Total current liabilities		**5,000**	
	Net current assets (CA − CL)			**16,300**
	Total assets			**40,300**
Long-term borrowings, mortgages, bank loans, etc	*Less creditors over one year*			*4,860*
	Net total assets			**35,440**
Funds invested and profits retained that belong to shareholders (owners)	**Shareholder's funds**			
	Initial capital introduced		*0*	
	Reserves (retained profits)		*35,400*	
	Total shareholder's' funds			**35,440**

business plan, it is viewed by anyone putting money into a business as essential. While the profit and loss account looks at economic activity over a period of time – a month, quarter or year – the balance sheet summarises the business's assets and liabilities at a particular point in time, usually the year end.

Table 10.5 shows a balance sheet built up from the information derived from the cashflow and profit and loss account in Tables 10.1 and 10.3. The equipment bought in is shown as fixed assets, as it has a life over one year. Taking off the depreciation leaves the net book value of the asset.

The working capital refers to short-term assets and liabilities such as debtors, customers who owe you money and stock you expect to shift in the future. Short term is defined as with the trading period of one year. Total assets are the sum of fixed assets and the working capital to which are added any long-term borrowings to arrive at the net total assets employed. That figure is balanced by the amount of money the shareholders have at stake.

🔆 JARGON BUSTER

Don't expect the accounting use of a term to necessarily correspond with its everyday use. For example, 'net book value' sounds like an estimate of the real value, but here it simply means the cost of the asset not yet depreciated. The actual value of the asset will almost certainly be a different figure altogether.

Balance sheets have to balance. Any change in any one area has at least two effects that keep it in balance. For example, if you find that you actually made a bit more profit than you at first thought, say 1,000, the reserves and cash go up by 1,000 each working through to a new balance of 36,440 of net total assets and of total shareholder's funds.

Your business plan should contain a summarised balance sheet in the body of the plan, covering a period of at least three years (Table 10.6 over the page). A more detailed account should be included in an appendix.

Estimating your break-even point

🔆 JARGON BUSTER

The stage at which income exceeds cost is the break-even point, and the period of time taken to reach that point is when anyone investing or lending money is at greatest risk.

TABLE 10.6: *Summarised three-year balance sheet*

Balance sheet at 31 March	Year 1	Year 2	Year 3
Fixed assets			
Less depreciation			
Net book value			
Current assets			
Stock			
Debtors			
Cash			
Total current assets			
Less current liabilities			
Overdraft			
Creditors			
Total current liabilities			
Net current liabilities			
Total assets			
Less creditors over one year			
Net total assets			
Shareholder's funds			
Initial capital introduced			
Reserves (retained profits)			
Total shareholder's funds			

Your business plan should show how long it will take you to reach break-even. As a rule of thumb, anything longer than 18 months would be a concern to backers as a lot can happen over that time. New competitors could enter the market, better products and services could come along or the market may turn sour.

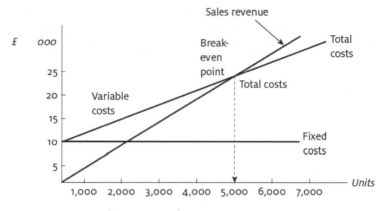

Figure 10.2 Break-even graph

First you need to distinguish between different types of cost. Some costs don't change, however much you sell: rent, rates and general utilities, for example. On the other hand, the cost of making the products you are selling, such as raw materials, distribution and sales commission, are all dependent on volume. The more you sell, the more it 'costs' to buy stock. The former of these costs is called 'fixed' and the latter 'variable', and you cannot add them together to arrive at total costs until you have made some assumptions about sales.

Figure 10.2 shows the factors that govern how break-even is achieved. The vertical axis shows the value of sales and costs in £000 and the horizontal axis the number of 'units' sold. In this elementary example, a business plans to sell only one product and has only one fixed cost, the annual rent and business rates, a total of £10,000. That is shown on the figure as a horizontal line above the axis. The angled line running from the top of the fixed costs line represents the variable costs. In this example, we plan to buy in at £3 per unit, so every unit we sell adds that much to our costs so that line also represents our total costs.

Only one element is needed to calculate the break-even point – the sales line. That is the line moving up at an angle from the bottom left-hand corner of the chart. We plan to sell out at £5 per unit, so this line is calculated by multiplying the units sold by that price.

The break-even point is the stage at which a business starts to make a profit. That is when the sales revenue begins to exceed both the fixed and variable costs. The chart shows our example break-even point as 5,000 units.

A formula, deduced from the chart, will save time for your own calculations:

$$\text{Break-even point} = \frac{\text{Fixed costs}}{\text{Selling price} - \text{Unit variable cost}}$$

$$\frac{10,000}{£5 - £3} = 5,000 \text{ units}$$

The next (and perhaps most important) calculation from a business planning perspective is to estimate when we will reach our break-even point. If our plan indicates that we will sell around 1,000 units a month, then it will take five months to reach break-even.

To complete the break-even picture we need to add one further dimension – your profit objective. In this example, £4,000 is used.

The new equation to include your 'desired' profit will look like this:

$$\text{Break-even profit point (BEPP)} = \frac{\text{Fixed costs} + \text{Profit objective}}{\text{Selling price} - \text{Unit variable cost}}$$

$$= \frac{10,000 + 4,000}{5 - 3} = 7,000 \text{ units}$$

We know that to reach our objective we must sell 7,000 units at £5 each and have no more than £10,000 tied up in fixed costs.

Using ratios

If you were thinking of buying a new car one of the factors you would take into consideration would be its MPG (miles per gallon). MPG is a ratio expressing the relationship between miles travelled and gallons of fuel used. It's a shorthand way to measure efficiency and running costs. It doesn't tell you everything, but it lets you compare one car with another, or one driver with another using the same car. You could also use it as a quick check to see if the engine appears to be getting less efficient over time.

> **Startups Tip**
> Ratios will give you a good feel for whether to go ahead with your plans or if you have more work to do on your strategic thinking.

Anyone reading a business plan will take a similar approach, using a number of ratios to form a view as to the viability and financial attractiveness of your venture. These are the key ratios that will be used and that you should include in your financial summary.

Levels of profit

Look back to Table 10.3, where you can see an example profit performance in some detail. Using those figures the following ratios are calculated below.

Gross profit

This is calculated by dividing the gross profit by sales and multiplying by 100. In this example the sum is 64,000/79,000 × 100 = 81%. This is a measure of the value being adding to the bought-in materials and services we need to 'make' our product or service; the higher the figure the better.

Operating profit

This is calculated by dividing the operating profit by sales and multiplying by 100. In this example the sum is 57,300/79,000 × 100 = 73%. This is a measure of how efficiently we are running the business, before taking account of financing costs and tax. These are excluded as interest and tax rates change periodically and are outside our direct control. Excluding them makes it easier to compare one period with another, or with another business. Once again the rule here is the higher the figure the better.

Net profit before and after tax

This is calculated by dividing the net profit before and after tax by the sales and multiplying by 100. In this example the sums are 44,300/79,000 × 100 = 56% and 35,440/79,000 × 100 = 45%. This is a measure of how efficiently we are running the business, after taking account of financing costs and tax. The last figure shows how successful we are at creating additional money to either invest back in the business or distribute to the owner(s) as either drawings or dividends. Once again the rule here is the higher the figure the better.

Working capital relationships

The money tied up in day-to-day activities is known as working capital, the sum of which is arrived at by subtracting the current liabilities from the current assets. In the example in Table 10.5, we have £21,300 in current assets and £5,000 in current liabilities, so the working capital is £16,300.

Current ratio

As a figure the working capital doesn't tell us much. It is rather as if you knew your car had used 20 gallons of petrol but had no idea how far you had travelled. It would be more helpful to know how much larger the current assets are than the current liabilities. That would give us some idea if the funds would be available to pay bills for stock, the tax liability and any other short-term liabilities that may arise. The current ratio, which is arrived at by dividing the current assets by the current liabilities, is the measure used. In this example the figures are 21,300/5,000 = 4.26. The convention is to express this as 4.26:1 and the aim here is to have a ratio of between 1.5:1 and 2:1. Any lower and bills can't be met easily; much higher and money is being tied up unnecessarily.

Return on capital employed (ROCE)

The fundamental financial purpose in business is to make a satisfactory return on the funds invested. ROCE is reputed to be one of Warren

Buffett's favourite ratios. This is calculated as a percentage in the same way as the interest you would get on any money on deposit in a bank is calculated. In this example, £34,440 is tied up in the business from various sources including the bank, to generate an operating profit of £57,300, that is profit before we pay the bank interest on money owed or tax. The return is calculated as 56,399/34,440 × 100 = 163.7%. This is a high figure by any standards. Only a handful of companies achieve this sort of return. Apple's five-year ROCE is just under 40%, IBM's 17% and Tesco's 16%.

Gearing

> ### 💡 JARGON BUSTER
>
> Gearing is the proportion of debt a business has compared to equity.
> Equity means all the funds put up by shareholders and includes both their investment and the profits retained in the business.

A business uses two fundamental types of money: debt, which has to be repaid, and equity, that is the money put in by the owners (shareholders). The relationship between the two is an important measure of a venture's riskiness. A high level of debt compared to equity is clearly a more risky proposition. Our example shows 4,860 of borrowings (debt) compared to 35,440 of shareholders' money in the business at the year end; that comes out at 13.71%. Anything up to around 50% would be seen as a reasonable ratio.

Alongside this ratio it is usual to show 'times interest earned', that is the number of times the operating profit covers the interest due on debt. That's similar to the ratio used in the mortgage market showing how many times your income covers the mortgage repayments. In this example the ratio is 57,300/1000 = 57.3 times. Anything above three times would generally be acceptable.

> ### ↻ Startups Tip
> Bookkeeping and accounting software often have 'report generator' programs that crunch out ratios for you, sometimes with helpful suggestions on areas to be probed further.

Keeping the books

The three accounting reports depend for their reliability on having a reliable bookkeeping/accounting system in place to record and analyse transactions. If you are in business, then include details of your financial team. If you are starting up in business, then your business plan should explain how you will keep the books.

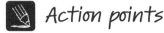 **Action points**

☑ Investigate reputable accounting software systems. You can get help in choosing software from Accounting Software Reviews (www.accounting-software-review. toptenreviews.com), which ranks the top 10 accounting packages priced from around £30 up to £1,500. Over 100 criteria are used in its tests, which it carries out yearly.

☑ Consider employing the services of a bookkeeper. Professional associations such as the International Association of Bookkeepers (IAB) (www.iab.org.uk) and the Institute of Certified Bookkeepers (www.book-keepers.org) offer free matching services to help small businesses find a bookkeeper to suit their particular needs. Expect to pay upwards of £20 an hour for services that can be as basic as simply recording the transactions in your books, through to producing accounts, preparing the value-added tax (VAT) return or doing the payroll. The big plus here is that a professional bookkeeper will have their own software.

☑ Explore the possibility of hiring an accountant to look after your books. Personal recommendation from someone in your business network is the best starting point to finding an accountant. Meet the person, and if you think you could work with him or her, take up references, as you *would with anyone you employ. Also, make sure he or she is a qualified member of one of the professional bodies, eg the Association of Chartered Certified Accountants (www.accaglobal.com) or the Institute of Chartered Accountants (www.icaewfirms.co.uk).*

Choosing the right software for your business can be an arduous task, and the section at Startups devoted to this topic (www.startups.co.uk/small-business-software) provides helpful tips on where to buy your software, keeping it up to date, saving money and what to look out for in terms of legal issues.

Getting the right bookkeeping system also is vital. The Startups section on bookkeeping (www.startups.co.uk/bookkeeping) covers everything you need to know about effective business bookkeeping.

Pulling it all together

Putting all your key data into a single table (such as Table 10.7 below) is a professional way to summarise the financial aspects of your business plan. You can include any back-up information, working documents and calculations in an appendix.

TABLE 10.7 Financial reports and controls – business plan summary

Profit levels		Year 1	Year 2	Year 3
	Sales turnover			
	Gross profit			
	Operating profit			
	Net profit			
Funds – uses and sources	Fixed assets			
	Working capital			
	Long-term borrowings			
	Shareholder's funds			

(Continued)

Performance ratios	Gross profit %			
	Operating profit %			
	Net profit before tax			
	Current ratio			
	ROCE			
	Gearing			
	Times interest earned			
Other accounting areas	Break-even	Volume to reach	Date to reach	
	Bookkeeping/ accounting	System used	Person responsible	

 Checklist

☑ Work out your cashflow until you reach a positive position.

☑ Prepare the balance sheets and profit and loss accounts for the period of the business plan.

☑ Calculate when you expect to achieve break-even.

☑ Calculate the key ratios for the performance indicated in your business plan.

☑ Identify a respected competitor and calculate as many of those ratios as you can from their accounts and compare your expected performance with their historic results.

☑ Consider what you can learn from your competitors' performance that will help you to improve your business plan.

CHAPTER 11
Raising funds

📖 What's in this chapter?

All business ventures need some cash to get going, and the more successful you are the more money you will need. Money will be required to buy in additional raw materials if you are selling products or to pay wages if you are in a service business. To remain competitive and visible your products and services will need modification and additions as will your website, all of which will call for more funds.

In this chapter we'll cover:

→ financing needs: when and how much

→ understanding the difference between borrowings and investments

→ sources of risk money – business angels, venture capitalists – and what they expect to see in your business plan

→ valuing your business

→ sources of funding.

Financing needs: when and how much

The cashflow projection (see Chapter 10) shows when and how much cash is required to meet the goals set out in your business plan. Table 11.1, a cut-down version of Table 10.1, shows the funding needs over the three months of the plan. Month one shows that 22,000 is required if the business is to stay liquid and be able to meet its obligations as they fall due. Month two shows the cash position improving, and at some point in the month the business has a positive cashflow. Based on these figures the business plan calls for 22,000 of funds to be in place for all of month one and in all probability for much of month two.

To allow for unforeseen problems and delays, in practice you would build in a margin of safety, depending on the circumstances and economic climate, and put a higher figure into your funding plan (there is more about this subject in Chapter 13 when we look at stress-testing). Also, remember it is always easier to raise more money than you need at the outset than going back to your funders for more. At the end of the day, prudence trumps optimism.

TABLE 11.1: *Estimating financing needs and timing*

	Month	One	Two	Three
		A	B	C
	Sales receipts			
	Cash sales	10,000	15,000	20,000
	Credit sales		10,000	12,000
1	**Total cash in**	**10,000**	**25,000**	**32,000**
	Payments			
2	Total cash out	32,000	18,200	12,500
3	Monthly cash surplus/deficit [1–2]	(22,000)	6,800	19,500
4	Cumulative cash surplus/deficit	(22,000)	(15,200) [3B–4A]	4,300 [3C–4B]

Nick Jenkins, Moonpig

Nick calculated he would need at least £200,000 to buy the necessary printer equipment and software – digital technology was still in development and an expensive proposition at the time. He would also need cash to pay for premises that were big enough to house the business.

Understanding the difference between borrowings and investments

Businesses have access to two fundamentally different sorts of money. The first, debt capital, is money borrowed by the business from banks and other lending institutions. In return for putting up the funds (or agreeing to make them available) lenders expect an interest payment over the life of the loan, irrespective of the performance of the business. In theory, lenders expect the money back at some time in the future; in practice, loans are usually revolved and replaced by another loan, perhaps for a different amount and on new terms.

Investment capital provided by venture capital firms and similar institutions is quite a different proposition. This type of funding is put up in return for a stake in the business. Unlike lenders who, irrespective of the success of the business, are limited to receiving an agreed level of interest in return for putting up the funds, investors have an unlimited upside. These firms become fellow shareholders and as such are entitled to a share of all the profits when they come through.

Sources of risk money – business angels, venture capitalists – and what they expect to see in your business plan

If you are operating as a limited company or limited partnership (see Chapter 12 where these terms are explained), you will have the opportunity to raise relatively risk-free money. It is risk free to the business that is, but risky to anyone taking a stake in the business should it not perform as expected.

Business angels or corporates such as venture capital providers share all the risks and vagaries of the business and expect a proportionate share in the rewards if things go well. They are not especially concerned with a stream of dividends nor do they look for the security of buildings or other assets to underpin their investment. Instead they hope for a radical increase in the value of their investment. They expect to realise this value from other investors who want to take their place for the next stage in the business's growth cycle. The assurance that outside investors will get the returns they are looking for has to be provided in the business plan.

Business angels

One likely first source of equity or risk capital will be a private individual with his or her own funds, and perhaps some knowledge of your type of business. In return for a share in the business, such investors will put in money at their own risk. They have been christened 'business angels', a term first coined to describe the private wealthy individuals who back a play on Broadway or in London's West End.

Business angels will probably know something about the sector you are working in, so expect elements of your business plan, particularly the marketing and competitor aspects, to be probed professionally. Angels usually want some involvement beyond merely signing a cheque and may expect to play a part in the business in some way. They are hoping for big rewards – one angel who backed Sage with £10,000 in its first round of £250,000 financing saw his stake rise to £40 million.

Angels can make decisions quickly and with the minimum of formality: it is their own money at stake. These angels frequently operate through managed networks, usually on the internet. The UK Business Angels Association (www.ukbusinessangelsassociation.org.uk) has an online directory of UK business angels. The European Business Angels Network (www.eban.org) has directories of national business angel associations both inside and outside of Europe from which you can find individual business angels.

> ### In my experience
>
> ### Edwina Dunn and Clive Humby, dunnhumby
>
> "We presented our business plan to some of our industry contacts, including Geoffrey Squire, CEO of Oracle UK at the time and an angel investor. He had been a colleague in our previous business and was so impressed he invested £250,000."

Venture capital/private equity

Venture capital providers are investing other people's money, often from pension funds. They have a different agenda from that of business angels, and are more likely to be interested in investing more money for a larger stake.

Firebox.com's co-creator (and founder of Mind Candy), Michael Smith, offers this advice on giving yourself a better chance with investors: "Raising money is tough, and as an entrepreneur you need to be aware of a whole host of things. One thing that's often overlooked is the state of the wider market. There are times every now and then when it's an entrepreneur's market to raise money, and we've seen that over the last year or two, but that's changing and the balance of power is shifting back to investors. Another is to make sure you have a great network, and this goes back to going to events, making sure you know other entrepreneurs. A great hook into investors is to become friendly with entrepreneurs they've invested in; that entrepreneur at the right time can introduce you to the investor. It's very very hard to just go cold into an investor that you don't know about; most of their deals come from trusted people that they know within their network. Also, do your homework: research everything that you can about that firm."

Venture capitalists go through a process known as 'due diligence' before investing.

JARGON BUSTER

This process involves a thorough examination of both the business and its owners. Past financial performance, the directors' track record and the business plan are all subjected to detailed scrutiny, usually by accountants and lawyers. Directors are then required to 'warrant' that they have provided all relevant information, under pain of financial penalties. The cost of this process will have to be borne by the firm raising the money, but it will be paid out of the money raised, if that is any consolation.

In general, venture capitalists expect their investment to have paid off within seven years, but they are hardened realists. Two in every 10 investments they make are total write-offs, and six perform averagely well at best. So, the one star in every 10 investments they make has to cover a lot of duds. Venture capitalists have a target rate of return of 30% plus, to cover this poor hit rate.

Raising venture capital is not a cheap option, and deals are not quick to arrange either. Six months is not unusual, and deals made over a year have been known. Every venture capitalist has a deal done in six weeks in its portfolio, but that truly is the exception.

Finding venture capital

Startups Tip

You can see how those negotiating with (or receiving) venture capital rate the firm in question at The Funded website (www.thefunded.com) in terms of the deal offered, the firm's apparent competence and how good they are managing the relationship. The Funded has over 2,000 members.

The British Venture Capital Association (www.bvca.co.uk) and the European Venture Capital Association (www.evca.com) both have online directories giving details of hundreds of venture capital providers. The Australian government (www.austradeict.gov.au/Globl-VC-directory/default.aspx) has a global venture capital directory on this website and the National Venture Capital Association (www.nvca.org) in the USA has directories of international venture capital associations both inside and outside that country.

In my experience

Nick Jenkins, Moonpig

Nick ploughed £160,000 of his own money into the business and raised a further £125,000 from three friends who were keen to invest. The three friends were all experienced investors and sufficiently wealthy for it not to be an issue if the business collapsed. This was perfect for Nick who wanted to get the website off the ground before securing venture capital, as having a product and customers would make the business a more attractive investment.

Corporate venturing

Some businesses invest in other firms in related industries. These firms, known as corporate venturers, usually want an inside track to new developments in and around the edges of their own fields of interest. For example, Cisco and Apple have billions invested in hundreds of small entrepreneurial businesses, taking stakes from a few hundred thousand dollars up to hundreds of millions. Microsoft's corporate venture arm was an early Facebook backer, putting up $240 million back in 2007.

And it's not just high-tech businesses that take this approach. McDonald's held a 35% stake in Prêt-à-Manger while they worked out where to take their business after saturating the burger market. (Only large cash-rich businesses have corporate venture arms.)

> ### Startups Tip
> Your business plan should show the value a corporate venture firm could get from investing in your business in terms of know-how, intellectual property, market intelligence or in some other material respect.

Valuing your business

Investors will assign a value to your business as the basis for deciding how big a shareholding they should get for money. The simplest and most usual way for businesses to be valued is using a formula known as the price/earnings (P/E) ratio. The P/E ratio is calculated by dividing the share price into the amount of profit earned for each share. For example, if a business makes £100,000 profit and has 1,000 shares, the profit per share is £100. If the share price of that company is £10, then its P/E ratio is 10 (100/10). You can check out the P/E for your business sector either by looking in *The Financial Times* or a similar newspaper.

Private companies don't have a quoted share price so the sector P/E is of limited use in arriving at a value. If a public company in your sector is on a P/E of 12, as a private company your prospective P/E would be around 8, or a third less. Why? Good question. The simplest answer is that while shares in your business are hard to dispose, you can unload a public company every business day by calling your broker. In other words, the premium is for liquidity.

> ### Startups Tip
> If you are looking for risk capital investment, your business plan should demonstrate that you have put a realistic and soundly calculated valuation on the business.

BDO Stoy Hayward's (www.bdo.co.uk) Private Company Price Index (PCPI) tracks the relationship between the current FTSE P/E ratio and the P/Es currently being paid on the sale of private companies. Put simply, the PCPI lets a company without a stock market listing get a reasonable idea of what it will actually sell for now.

In my experience

Nick Jenkins, Moonpig

"Completing several rounds of financing taught me some important lessons, not least how to structure a deal. From experience I believe that it can be all too easy to give away too much company equity in the early days."

Sources of funding

Bank finance

Banks are the principal (and frequently only) source of finance for nine out of every 10 business propositions. They provide a spectrum of loans, from short-term overdrafts that are technically repayable on demand, to long-term loans. Bankers, and indeed any other sources of debt capital, are looking for asset security to back their loan and provide a near certainty of getting their money back. They will also charge an interest rate that reflects current market conditions and their view of the risk level of the proposal.

Bankers like to speak of the 'five Cs' of credit analysis, factors they look at when they evaluate a loan request. When applying to a bank for a loan, your business plan should address the following specific points:

⇀ **Character:** bankers lend money to borrowers who appear honest and who have a good credit history. Before you apply for a loan, it makes sense to obtain a copy of your credit report and clean up any problems.

⇀ **Capacity:** this is a prediction of the borrower's ability to repay the loan. For a new business, bankers look at the business plan. For an existing business, bankers require a business plan and will also consider past financial statements and current market conditions.

⟿ **Collateral:** bankers generally want a borrower to pledge an asset that can be sold to pay off the loan if the borrower lacks funds.

⟿ **Capital:** bankers don't like to get involved in businesses where the debt to equity ratio is too high (see Chapter 10).

⟿ **Conditions:** whether bankers give a loan can be influenced by the current economic climate as well as by the amount.

> ### Startups Tip
> All businesses need to deal with the bank at some point. Even if your business does not need a loan or overdraft, you will still need a business bank account to make and receive payments. The Startups section on this topic (www.startups.co.uk/banks-and-loans) covers everything from how to select a business bank account and bank manager, to how to present your business when trying to obtain a bank loan.

Sportingbet.com's founder, Mark Blandford, has this advice to offer on not accepting a 'No' from a bank manager: "My betting shop career nearly didn't get off the ground at all thanks to a Mr Jones at Barclays Bank in Broad Street, Hereford. He decided that it wasn't a good idea, and although I'd banked with him for some eight or 10 years, he wasn't going to lend me the money. It was a fairly short and frank conversation. Through good fortune I got introduced to another bank manager who, luckily for me (and perhaps luckily for him), took a different view. That enabled me to buy my first betting shop and that was it really."

Leasing and hire purchase

Though you don't require a business plan to raise this type of funding, anyone else you are pitching to will expect you to have built these options into your proposition. Physical assets such as cars, vans, computers, office equipment and the like can usually be financed by leasing them, rather as a house or flat may be rented.

In my experience

Edwina Dunn and Clive Humby, dunnhumby

"We approached banks and private investors, and while all of them were willing to invest in the business, this was on the condition that they owned a majority stake in dunnhumby after the business had been running for three years. After some consideration we decided not to accept any other investment as we weren't prepared to sacrifice our ownership of the business. It seemed silly that in three years' time, after working hard to get the business off the ground, we wouldn't even own the majority of it."

Alternatively, they can be bought on hire purchase. This leaves other funds free to cover the less tangible elements in your business plan.

Leasing is a way of getting the use of vehicles, plant and equipment without paying the full cost all at once. Operating leases are taken out where you will use the equipment (eg a car, photocopier, vending machine or kitchen equipment) for less than its full economic life. The lessor takes the risk of the equipment becoming obsolete, and assumes responsibility for repairs, maintenance and insurance. As you, the lessee, are paying for this service, it is more expensive than a finance lease, where you lease the equipment for most of its economic life and maintain and insure it yourself. Leases can normally be extended, often for fairly nominal sums, in the latter years.

Hire purchase differs from leasing in that you have the option to eventually become the owner of the asset, after a series of payments.

Startups Tip

The Finance and Leasing Association (www.fla.org) gives details of all UK-based businesses offering this type of finance. The website also has general information on terms of trade and codes of conduct.

> ### Startups Tip
> Bank loans and overdrafts are not the only way to free up cash for your business. Unpaid invoices and business assets can also be used to secure cash advances. The Startups section on this topic (www.startups.co.uk/asset-based-lending) looks at asset-based lending such as invoice financing and factoring, how it all works and whether it is suitable for your business.

Grant aid and other free money sources

As with leasing and hire purchase, anyone lending or investing in a business will expect your business plan to show that any prospective grant or other free money source has at least been investigated. You can't run the risk of a financier knowing more than you do about your business sector as that would seriously undermine the credibility of your proposition. In any event, most forms of relatively free money require a business plan to access them.

Your business plan will need to build in any specific requirements and conditions imposed as a term of the grant. For example, grants can be conditional on job creation, location, investment in training, taking on young workers or recent graduates or developing specific processes or technologies.

> ### Startups Tip
> They are not easy to come by, but there are a lot of different business grants out there covering all kinds of business sectors. Some are given out to entrepreneurs who meet certain criteria, while others focus on the type of business being started. The Startups section on this topic (www.startups.co.uk/grants_1) covers everything you need to know about how to apply for a business grant and, more importantly, where to look for them.

Crowdfunding

Crowdfunding business finance is a new, game-changing concept that puts the power firmly into the hands of entrepreneurs looking to raise finance. Instead of one large investor putting money into a business, larger numbers of smaller investors contribute as little as £10 each to raise the required capital. Crowd Cube, the first UK-based crowdfunding website, has now teamed up with Startups.co.uk so entrepreneurs will be able to both access information on raising finance and have direct access to an innovative way to solve the problem from one site (www.crowdcube.com/partner/startups).

Crowdcube is the first crowdfunding website in the world to enable the public to invest in and receive shares in UK companies, and has more than 7,000 registered members currently seeking investment opportunities. The platform has already raised more than £2 million for small businesses through its principal site, and hosted the world's first £1 million crowdfunding deal in November 2011. The range of businesses that have used this financing method is wide and getting wider. Darlington Football Club raised £291,450 from 722 investors over 14 days through the crowdfunding website Crowdcube to help fend off closure after going into liquidation. Oil supplier Universal Fuels has raised £100,000 through the same crowdfunding platform, making founder Oliver Morgan the youngest entrepreneur to successfully raise investment through the process.

Enterprise finance guarantee

If your business plan looks like delivering neither the fast growth required by investors nor the security that lenders look for, the government's enterprise finance guarantee (EFG) is a possibility. The EFG facilitates bank lending of between £1,000 and £1 million to viable businesses with an annual turnover up to £25 million, but which lack the security to secure a normal commercial loan. The government provides the lender with a guarantee for which the borrower pays a premium. Accredited lenders make all decisions on lending rather than the Department for Business Innovation and Skills, which administers the EFG (see www.bis.gov.uk/policies/enterprise-and-business-support/access-to-finance/enterprise-finance-guarantee).

> **Startups Tip**
> Check out the Startups website (www.startups.co.uk) for the latest information on bank, venture capital, business angel and corporate venture funding, and more.

 **Checklist**

☑ Estimate how much funding your business plan calls for by preparing a projection using Table 11.1 as a guide.

☑ Identify the venture capital firms, business angels or organisations with an interest in corporate venturing which operate in your business sector.

☑ Consider how you can demonstrate in your business plan that you can meet a lender's five Cs criteria.

☑ Identify what grant aid is available in your sector.

☑ Consider whether you would be better advised to put your business plan to a crowdfunding or EFG provider.

⤳ **CHAPTER 12**
Legal and tax matters

📖 What's in this chapter?

From the outset, any business is constrained by rules and regulations. Your access to funding will be dependent on the legal structure of the business, and to some extent by the ownership split of shares in the case of companies. Your capacity to generate income will be directly affected by your ability to get any permissions required to trade, and cashflow projections will need to reflect any relevant costs and the timings of events caused by tax, which can have 'lumpy' characteristics, with large sums going out quarterly or half yearly.

In this chapter we'll cover:

-↦ business structure: sole trader, partnership or limited company
-↦ accounting for tax and VAT
-↦ areas that affect cashflow and profitability
-↦ auditing and filing your accounts
-↦ keeping investors and lenders informed.

Business structure: sole trader, partnership or limited company

Your business plan should state what legal form your business will take. There are three main forms, and the one you choose will depend on a number of factors: commercial needs, financial risk and tax position. Each of these forms is explained briefly below, together with the procedure to follow when setting them up. You can change your ownership status later as your circumstances change, so while this is an important decision it is not a final one.

Limited company

A limited company has the ability to sell off parts of itself by way of shares and so raise money – an essential feature if your business plan is going to be seen by any source of venture capital (see Chapter 11). Companies have a legal identity of their own, separate from the people who own or run them. This means that, in the event of failure, creditors' claims are restricted to the assets of the company. The shareholders of the business are not liable as individuals for the business debts beyond the paid-up value of their shares. This applies even if the shareholders are working directors, unless of course the company has been trading fraudulently. (In practice, the ability to limit liability is severely restricted these days as most lenders, including banks, often insist on personal guarantees from the directors.) Other advantages include the freedom to raise capital by selling shares.

Disadvantages include the cost involved in setting up the company and the legal requirement in some cases for the company's accounts to be audited by a chartered or certified accountant. Usually it is only businesses with assets approaching £3m that have to be audited but if, for example, you have shareholders who own more than 10% of your business, they can ask for the accounts to be audited. You can find out the latest information on auditing small business either from your accountant or on www.gov.uk.

A limited company can be formed by two shareholders, one of whom must be a director. A company secretary must also be appointed, who can be a shareholder, director or an outside person, such as an accountant or lawyer.

You can form a company yourself, online, for about £20, or buy one 'off the shelf' from a registration agent, then adapt to suit your own purposes. This will involve changing the name, shareholders and articles of association, and will cost about £250 (taking a couple of weeks to arrange). Alternatively, you can form your own company, using your solicitor or accountant. This will cost around £700 and take six to eight weeks.

Your business plan should include information on who the shareholders will be, what proportion of shares they have and details of any share option schemes to be used to incentivise staff.

> **Startups Tip**
> Check out the Startups website (www.startups.co.uk/setting-up-a-company) for a step-by-step guide to forming a limited company, a rundown of the different organisations that can deal with all the paperwork for you and the documents you need to submit to register your company.

Partnerships

Partnerships are effectively collections of sole traders (see below) and, as such, share the legal problems attached to personal liability. There are very few restrictions to setting up in business with another person (or persons) in partnership, and several definite advantages. By pooling resources you may have more capital; you will be bringing, hopefully, several sets of skills to the business; and if you are ill the business can still carry on: all factors anyone reading your business plan will see as valuable benefits.

There are two serious drawbacks, however, that you should certainly consider. First, every member of a partnership must shoulder the consequences of adverse financial events, so your personal assets could be taken to pay the creditors even though the mistake was no fault of your own. Secondly, if your partner goes bankrupt in his or her personal capacity, for whatever reason, his or her share of the partnership can be seized by creditors.

The legal regulations governing this field are set out in the Partnership Act 1890, which in essence assumes that competent business people should know what they are doing. The Act merely provides a framework of agreement that applies 'in the absence of agreement to the contrary'. It follows from this that many partnerships are entered into without legal formalities – and sometimes without the parties themselves being aware that they have entered a partnership!

The main provisions of the Partnership Act state:

- all partners contribute capital equally
- all partners share profits and losses equally
- no partner shall have interest paid on their capital
- no partner shall be paid a salary
- all partners have an equal say in the management of the business.

It is unlikely that all these provisions will suit you, so you would be well advised to get a 'partnership agreement' drawn up in writing by a solicitor at the outset. In any event, your business plan should detail who your partners are, what role they will play in the business and provide sufficient information on their business experience to give a lender comfort.

> **Startups Tip**
> Check out the Startups website (www.startups.co.uk/partnerships) for information on how to structure your partnership and some basic rules for avoiding disaster.

Sole trader

Over 80% of businesses start up as sole traders, and indeed around 55% of all businesses employing fewer than 50 people still use this legal structure. It has the merit of being relatively free of formality and cost free. There is no requirement for your accounts to be audited, or for financial information on your business to be filed at Companies House.

As a sole trader, there is no legal distinction between you and your business – your business is one of your assets, just as your house or car is. It follows from this that if your business should fail, your creditors have a right not only to the assets of the business but also to your personal assets, subject only to the provisions of the Bankruptcy Acts (these allow you to keep only a few absolutely basic essentials for yourself and family). The capital to get the business going must come from you, or from loans as there is no access to equity capital (see Chapter 11 for more on equity).

> ### Startups Tip
> Check out the Startups website (www.startups.co.uk/registering-as-a-sole-trader_1), as although simple to set up, there are legal issues of which you need to be aware. Use the Startups step-by-step guide to registering as self-employed.

Accounting for tax and VAT

If you are already trading, this subject will be familiar territory. In any event, your business plan should show the effect of tax and VAT on your projected profits and cashflow, as these are often the largest area of expense. You should also show that you understand the tax regime and how to operate within the law, while incurring the least unnecessary expense.

The letter of the law

The challenge for directors and managers is to recognise the distinction between different types of behaviour when it comes to tax law.

–‍> **Tax fraud:** this is often called tax evasion to soften the underlying meaning. This involves the intentional behaviour or actual knowledge of the wrongdoing, for example reducing the tax burden by underreporting income, overstating deductions or using illegal tax shelters; this is a criminal matter.

–‍> **Tax mitigation:** this involves the taxpayer taking advantage of a fiscally attractive option afforded to them by the tax legislation and 'genuinely suffers the economic consequences that Parliament intended to be suffered by those taking advantage of the option', as stated one Law Lord summing up the subject. So, for example, if a business is allowed to offset the cost of an asset against tax, so long as they actually buy the asset they are mitigating their tax position.

–‍> **Tax avoidance:** this lies in the blurred line between tax mitigation and tax fraud and is usually defined by the test of whether your dominant purpose – or your sole purpose – was to reduce or eliminate tax liability.

Taxation

> **Startups Tip**
> You can find out more about all aspects of business tax at the Startups website (www.startups.co.uk/small-business-tax).

Businesses have three main operating taxes to account for. Their effect on both cashflow and profit can be significant and your business plan should incorporate how you intend to deal with all three.

Tax on profits

The purchase of capital items such as plant, machinery and equipment, buildings and any such long-term assets are treated for tax purposes in a particular manner. In the profit and loss account these costs are usually shown as an item of depreciation spread over the working life of the asset(s) concerned. In Table 10.3, Chapter 10, you will see that 12,000 has been deducted for that purpose before the taxable profit is arrived at. For tax purposes, however, depreciation is not an allowable expense, rather it is replaced with a 'writing down allowance' (see

Table 12.1 below), the amount of which varies according to the policies favoured by the government of the day.

Table 12.1 adds in two further columns to allow for depreciation to be replaced with a writing down allowance. In the example we have assumed that the 36,000 of cash spent on equipment (see Table 10.1) is 100% allowable for tax purposes. While this may be an exaggeration, it is not unusual for this level of first year capital allowance to be in force. Now you can see that the tax bill has been more than halved. While the after profits are lower, a necessary condition if the tax bill is to be reduced, the business now still has assets on the books at 24,000 (see Table 10.5), fully depreciated. So next year's profits will be correspondingly higher, but the business has had the advantage of a lower tax expense in the first year of trading or of pursuing a strategy of expansion.

TABLE 12.1: Effect of writing down allowance on business tax

Profit and loss account for year ended 20XX		Tax adjusted profit and loss account for 20XX	
Operating profit	57,300	Operating profit	57,300
Less	.	Less	
Interest on borrowings	1,000	Interest on borrowings	1,000
Depreciation	12,000	Writing down allowance	36,000
Profit before tax	44,300	Profit before tax	20,300
Tax at 20%	8,860		4,060
Net profit after tax	35,440		16,240

Employment taxes

Employers are responsible for collecting tax and a National Insurance contribution from their employees and paying that over to HM Revenue and Customs (HMRC). This could in effect give a company a short-term cashflow benefit if there is a time lag between making deductions from employees' wages and passing the money to HMRC. The cashflow projections and profit and loss accounts used in your business plan should include details and timings of these collections and payments, although the net effect is neutral as employers are only paying over the sums they collect.

Value added tax

VAT is a tax most suppliers of goods and services charge by adding it to those goods and services. Businesses with annual turnover in excess of £77,000 have to register, but you can register at any stage and may find a short-term cashflow advantage from doing so.

> **Startups Tip**
>
> It is essential that, as a business owner, you understand the ins and outs of National Insurance contributions and PAYE. Every business has to abide by government regulations and pay the correct amount, and the Startups website (www.startups.co.uk/national-insurance-and-paye) provides crucial information and helpful tips for small businesses, indicating the different rates they should pay.

Table 12.2 on the next page shows the theoretical cashflow advantage the business used as an example in Chapter 10 could have by registering for VAT, despite being below the threshold where registration is compulsory. The business becomes net cashflow positive in the second period rather than the third and has the use of up to 13,400 of VAT collected for some or all of the three periods prior to paying it over.

Areas that affect cashflow and profitability

There are a number of areas that can have a significant effect on financial performance, and your business plan should explain how you intend to treat them.

Licences and permits

Some businesses, such as those working with food or alcohol, employment agencies, mini-cabs and hairdressers, need a licence or permit before they can set up in business at all. You should accommodate the cost of such a licence and any likely delay in

TABLE 12.2: Possible cashflow benefits from registering for VAT

Cashflow forecast	Not registered for VAT			Registered for VAT		
Month	April	May	June	April	May	June
	A	B	C	AA	BB	CC
Sales receipts						
Cash sales	10,000	15,000	20,000	10,000	15,000	20,000
Credit sales		10,000	12,000		10,000	12,000
VAT collected				2,000	5,000	6,400
1 Total cash in	**10,000**	**25,000**	**32,000**	**12,000**	**30,000**	**38,400**
Payments						
Salary, materials etc	32,000	18,200	12,500	32,000	18,200	12,500
VAT paid to HMRC	–	–	–	–	–	13,400
2 Total cash out	**32,000**	**18,200**	**12,500**	**32,000**	**18,200**	**25,900**
3 Monthly cash surplus/ deficit [1–2]	**(22,000)**	**6,800**	**19,500**	**(20,000)**	**11,800**	**12,500**
4 Cumulative cash surplus/ deficit	(22,000)	(15,200) [3B–4A]	4,300 [3C–4B]	(20,000)	8,200 [3BB–4AA]	4,300 [3CC–4BB]

being able to generate sales revenue into your cashflow forecast.
Your local authority planning department can advise you what
rules will apply to your business. You can also use the interactive tool
on www.gov.uk/licence-finder to find out which permits, licences and
registrations will apply and where to get more information.

If you plan to let your customers buy on credit or hire out or lease
products to private individuals or to businesses, then you will in all
probability have to apply to be licensed to provide credit. If you think
this could apply to your business, read the regulations on the website
of the Office of Fair Trading (www.oft.gov.uk).

Terms of trade

You need to decide on your terms and conditions of sale and ensure they are printed on your order acceptance stationery. Terms should include when and how you require to be paid, and under what conditions you will accept cancellations or offer refunds. The websites of the Office of Fair Trading (www.oft.gov.uk) and Trading Standards Central (www.tradingstandards.gov.uk) contain information on most aspects of trading relationships. The credit period you allow customers before should be factored into your cashflow and profit projections as should an allowance for returns or cancellations.

Checking creditworthiness

There is a wealth of information on credit status for both individuals and businesses of varying complexity at prices from £5 for basic information through to £200 for a very comprehensive picture of credit status. So there is no need to trade unknowingly with individuals or businesses that pose a credit risk.

The major agencies which compile and sell personal credit histories and small business information are Experian (www.UKexperian.com), Dun & Bradstreet (www.dnb.com), Creditgate.com (www.creditgate. com) and Credit Reporting (www.creditreporting.co.uk/b2b). Between them they offer a comprehensive range of online credit reports instantly, including advice on credit limit and CCJs.

> ### Startups Tip
> When running a business, there are important rules and regulations you must adhere to in order to satisfy the authorities. There are various employee laws (ranging from equal pay to flexible working) to bear in mind, while you can also use the law to your benefit, such as making a claim against a debtor. Visit Startups (www.startups.co.uk/legal-issues-and-red-tape) to keep up to date on these and other related issues.

Insurance

Anyone providing finance will expect some aspects of your business to carry insurance to protect their and your investment in the event of calamity. You should build these insurance costs into your business plan.

→ **Public liability:** this is compulsory and is intended to meet legal liability to customers and employees for death or injury on or around your premises.

→ **Product liability:** this protects customers from faulty goods, or any event related to your product or service which results in harm or expense. You could be at risk for anything you supply, whether or not you manufacture it.

→ **Property and equipment:** much as with your domestic arrangements, valuable assets should be insured.

→ **Loss of profits:** while property insurance covers the cost of replacing assets damaged or rendered unable to operate, it doesn't cover the loss of income from not being able to fulfil orders. For that you will need loss of profits insurance.

→ **Key Person Insurance:** your business is likely to rely heavily on one or two people, yourself included. If a key person becomes ill or dies there can be serious consequences for the business. Any bank, venture capital firm or business angel will want their investment protected against such an event.

→ **Professional Indemnity:** if your business involves selling your knowledge or skills, this insurance protects your business against claims for loss or damage made by a client or third party for your mistakes or negligence.

These are not all the risks that a business may have to insure against, but they are the ones most likely to feature in most business plans.

> ◠ **Startups Tip**
> Check out the Startups website (www.startups.co.uk/insurance)
> for information on all the different types of business insurance,
> including what you need to protect your business premises and
> equipment, as well as what you are legally required to have as a
> business owner and employer.

Auditing and filing your accounts

Investors and lenders reading your business plan will want to be
confident that you have made provisions to properly report on what
you have done with their money. In practice, this means explaining
how you will ensure the accounts for your business will be produced
to the required standard and on time. This is achieved by having the
accounts audited and then filed at the appropriate time at Companies
House. For unincorporated businesses the procedure is simpler, as all
that is usually required by a lender is to have your accounts signed off
by a qualified accountant.

The audit

Small companies with a turnover of not more than £5.6 million and
a balance sheet total of not more than £2.8 million don't need to
have an audit, though any business with outside shareholders will
almost certainly be expected to have one. The audit is the company
equivalent of an MOT. The purpose of the audit, which is carried out
annually, is to make sure the company has produced its accounts using
the prevailing accounting standards and principles and that the figures
give a 'true and fair' representation of the company's financial position.
In practice, in a small company the auditor will rely on the directors
supplying correct information and not deliberately concealing or
misrepresenting information. You can also expect an auditor to give
an opinion about the dependability and appropriateness of the
company's accounting methods and systems.

The directors appoint auditors for the first trading year. Once
the auditors have audited the company's accounts, the accounts

are presented to the shareholders by the directors. The shareholders can then decide to reappoint the auditors, or appoint different auditors, to hold office until the next accounts are presented and audited – and so on each year. Auditors have to be members of the major professional accounting bodies. Generally, cost will be a crucial factor for a private business in appointing auditors, unless they are looking specifically to create a degree of external respectability, for example if they are preparing to go public or raise large sums of new capital.

> **Startups Tip**
> You can keep track of who's who in the auditing world through Accountancy Age (www.accountancyage.com/resource/top50), which lists the major audit firms in rank order each year.

Filing the accounts

If you are trading as a company then you have to file your accounts with Companies House (www.companieshouse.gov.uk) each year. Unless you are filing your company's first accounts, the time normally allowed for delivering accounts to Companies House is 10 months from the end of the relevant accounting period for private companies. If you are filing your company's first accounts and they cover a period of more than 12 months, you must deliver them to the Registrar at Companies House within 22 months of the date of incorporation for private companies.

All companies must prepare full accounts for presentation to their shareholders, but small and medium-sized companies can send abbreviated accounts to the Registrar of Companies. Abbreviated accounts contain very little information that can be of use to a competitor. Nothing is given away on turnover or margins, for example, a luxury denied to larger companies. Small companies' accounts (ones with less than £5.6 million turnover, balance sheet total less than £2.8 million and fewer than 50 employees on average, to be precise) delivered to the Registrar must contain:

→ an abbreviated balance sheet

→ selected notes to the accounts, including accounting policies, share capital, particulars of creditors payable in more than five years, and the basis of any foreign currency transactions

→ a special auditor's report (unless exempt from audit).

> **Startups Tip**
> The rules of disclosure are complex, and this is only a brief outline of the requirements. If you're unsure about the information that you have to provide, you should take professional advice.

Keeping investors and lenders informed

> **Startups Tip**
> Unless you're an expert on taxation, you'll need to find a good accountant to help with your business's finances. Check out the Startups website (www.startups.co.uk/accountants) for tips on how to choose an accountant and agreeing the best terms for your business. The website also provides some useful contacts from the accountancy industry.

Your investors and lenders will want to know you have systems in place to keep them fully informed of the business's position throughout the year. While the audited annual accounts are the most reliable indication of how things are going, you should provide them with accounts each month. Whoever acts as your company accountant, be they a part-timer from outside, a fellow director or yourself, the task is to provide timely and appropriate financial information with which to run the business. This in practice means:

→ Your monthly management accounts should be available within a week of the end of each month. You have either the wrong accountant or the wrong accounting system if you cannot achieve this standard. If you don't yet have monthly management accounts, make that your accountant's next measurable goal.

⇥ Accounting systems and reports should be simple, free of jargon and supported by clear written explanations of the key issues to consider. For example, if profits are down by 10%, besides the bald figures, an explanation that this was caused by a 5% reduction in sales of product X and a 5% increase in raw material costs will give a clear indication of responsibilities and possible remedies.

⇥ Your accountant should also ensure that your books and records are kept to the standard required by company law. They must also see that your accounting policies meet the required standards and that accounts, VAT returns, PAYE and tax demands are dealt with in a timely manner.

In my experience

Nick Jenkins, Moonpig

"I needed to rewrite the business plan to show we wouldn't spend millions on land-grabbing marketing campaigns and would be smart in how we used investors' money."

HMRC expects VAT, tax and National Insurance contributions to be paid on time. Martin Webb, presenter of Channel 4's *Risking it All*, believes people spend too little time looking at their own figures. In his opinion "A lot of people take the view that you get your accounts audited once a year and let's see how much we've made. Getting an accountant to look at your accounts at the year-end is too late. You need to be doing weekly, bi-weekly, monthly profit and loss figures to see how you're doing, because if you are going wrong, if there is a problem, you need to be able to do something about it immediately and quickly. For a very small start-up business I would do a profit and loss every week, even if it's just a back-of-the-envelope exercise because then you can make sure you're covering your costs, you've got enough money to live on, you've got enough to pay your suppliers and you're putting enough aside for your VAT, National Insurance and tax if you're making a profit."

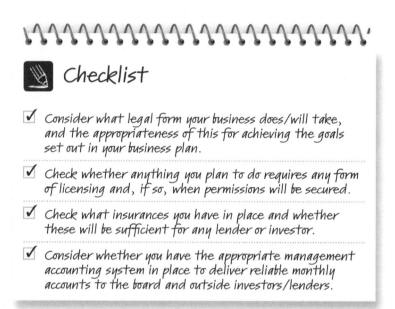

Checklist

☑ Consider what legal form your business does/will take, and the appropriateness of this for achieving the goals set out in your business plan.

☑ Check whether anything you plan to do requires any form of licensing and, if so, when permissions will be secured.

☑ Check what insurances you have in place and whether these will be sufficient for any lender or investor.

☑ Consider whether you have the appropriate management accounting system in place to deliver reliable monthly accounts to the board and outside investors/lenders.

↻ CHAPTER 13

Stress-testing your business model

📖 What's in this chapter?

Bankers, investors and partners are unlikely to take your plan at face value. They will be interested in probing for risk factors: things that could work against you under certain circumstances. What if – the economy turns sour, your patent takes longer to come through, sales take longer to take off than you have forecasted, etc? The questions are designed to assess the likely impact of these events on your cashflow. Remember, cash is king and without it no business can survive long enough to become profitable. The best framework for stress-testing your business model is the cashflow forecast, checking the impact of your key business planning assumptions being disrupted.

In this chapter we'll cover:

→ listing the key assumptions
→ using the cashflow model

→ stress-testing the revenue model

→ stress-testing the payments model

→ testing to destruction

→ holding a tiger by the tail

→ measuring milestones

→ reviewing the possibilities of insuring against risks.

Listing the key assumptions

Your business plan has been prepared with your view of what the future holds. Those assumptions, and the logic and evidence that underpin them, should be documented. These can be referred to in the body of your business plan and then consigned to an appendix alongside other items of important data, such as market research studies.

External assumptions

These are the factors that, though completely out of your control, will have a direct bearing on the performance your business plan is claiming to be attainable. PEST analysis is a tool used to categorise the external 'political', 'economic', 'social' and 'technological' factors that influence business thinking. Often two additional factors, 'environmental' and 'legal', are added, changing the acronym to PESTEL analysis (Table 13.1). This is basically a checklist to ensure that all major factors that could impact on a business are taken into consideration. The general economic environment of the countries you will be operating in should be top of your list of assumptions. For example, at the time of writing, the UK was expected to grow by between 1% and 2%, while growth in China and India was expected to be between 9% and 10%, over the following two years: that would suggest very different trading conditions.

Table 13.1 PESTEL analysis

Factor	Condition	Impact	Timing	Proposed response
Political				
Economic				
Social/cultural				
Technological				
Environmental				
Legal				

The state of the economy will affect many business areas. A booming economy could be good for sales but it may make it harder to recruit new staff.

James Caan, founder of private equity firm Hamilton Bradshaw, and a former star of *Dragons' Den*, has this advice for aspiring entrepreneurs putting together their first pitch: "Make it realistic, do your homework, understand your numbers and absolutely demonstrate your passion, your belief and your conviction as to why the investor should believe in you to deliver this plan."

Different types of businesses will be affected by different factors, and to differing degrees. For example, a real estate business would take into consideration economic factors such as likely local interest rates, the availability of funds, changes in capital gains and inheritance taxes brought about by, say, a new government, etc. Companies in the home improvements market might recognise growth opportunities when they see the vigour with which energy audits and compulsory water meters for all homes loom on the horizon.

The specific market conditions for your product or service should be included in your assumptions. They could be counter to the prevailing trend in the economy. The International Monetary Fund (IMF) produces regular economic forecasts for most countries (www. imf.org/external/data.htm) and the Trade Association Forum (www. taforum.org) is the directory of trade associations on whose websites are links to industry-relevant online research sources for data on market trends and conditions.

In my experience

Edwina Dunn and Clive Humby, dunnhumby

The fallout from the markets following the dotcom bust led to a recession, and although dunnhumby had been growing steadily over the years and making a profit every year, the business was badly affected. It was the worst chapter in the business's history.

Internal assumptions

These include factors over which you have a measure of control, for example when a new product or service should be ready, a website launched or updated, a supplier located, a licence applied for or a quality standard achieved. The list of these factors is potentially long, so concentrate only on the important factors relevant to your business over the period of your business plan.

Using the cashflow model

Generally, when people talk of business success, they have profit in mind. However, in accounting terms, profit is a matter as much of judgement as of fact. Table 13.2 shows the same set of accounts tabled using two different but realistic and acceptable assumptions.

Common to both assumptions is that sales turnover will be 20,000, based on using up 5,000 of materials with equipment costing 10,000.

Table 13.2 *Profit versus cash*

Profit and loss account			
Assumption 1		Assumption 2	
Sales turnover	20,000		20,000
Less material purchases	5,000		5,000
Depreciation of 10,000 equipment over two years	5,000	Depreciation of 10,000 equipment over five years	2,000
Total expenses	10,000		7,000
Profit	10,000		13,000
Cashflow			
Sales turnover	20,000		20,000
Less material purchases	5,000		5,000
and Cost of equipment	10,000	Equipment paid for in cash when bought	10,000
Net cashflow	5,000		5,000

Under assumption 1, the equipment is depreciated over two years so bringing a cost of 5,000 into the profit and loss account. The resulting profit is 10,000 (20,000 − 5,000 + 5,000). Assumption 2 has the equipment depreciated over five years so producing 13,000 of profit (20,000 − 5,000 +2,000). To keep the arithmetic simple we will assume that all sales are for cash and we pay our suppliers pro forma (on the nail). The cashflow picture under both assumptions is the same: the business will have 5,000 cash in the bank at the end of the period. That is the only real money available to the business to pay short-terms bills, wages, more materials, tax and so forth. Without that cash it can't go on. Assumption 2 could be perfectly realistic and is probably acceptable depending on the nature of the equipment. For stress-testing purposes, as with much else in business, cashflow is the measure used.

> ### Startups Tip
> A good place to find spreadsheets with 'what if' facilities is at Microsoft (www.office.microsoft.com/en-gb/templates/?CTT=97) entering Cash-flow in the search pane.

Stress-testing the revenue model

It is unlikely that anyone will take your sales revenue as read. The norm in business is for something to not go to plan. Either you get fewer customers, the mix of customers changes say from cash to credit, less repeat business occurs, your prices don't hold as expected or you get more returns or defects.

The list of reasons that could adversely hit your sales receipts is endless. Figure 13.1 shows the effect on cashflow in an example where sales revenue is 20% adrift from the figures projected in the business plan. It is always prudent to leave payments broadly similar despite a drop in sales, although logic suggests that some costs would fall. Variable costs (see Chapter 10), such as materials, should go down with sales volumes, but in practice you may buy in materials to meet the planned sales. In such cases you will use fewer materials and carry them over in stock for a later period. Nevertheless, your cash position will be much as if you had actually used those materials.

Category	Business Plan		Revenue
			What if
Sales receipts			
Cash sales	50000		40000
Credit sales	50000		40000
Total cash in	100000	Sales −20%	80000
Payments			
Salary and wages	25000		25000
Utilities	10000		10000
Rent and rates	15000		15000
Materials	35000		35000
Equipment	40000	Payments same	40000
Total cash out	125000		125000
Net cash flow	-25000		-45000
		Funding needs	
Funding needs	-25000	+20,000	-45000

Figure 13.1 Testing the revenue model

In Figure 13.1 you can see that under this 'what if' scenario the funding requirement goes up from 25,000 to 45,000.

Stress-testing the payments model

As with sales revenue, payments can take an unexpected turn for the worse. Inflationary pressures can push up wages and material costs. Utilities and motoring costs moved up by nearly 40% in the UK between 2008 and 2010. Figure 13.2 shows what would happen to cashflow if costs rise and sales revenue remains static. In this example an additional 17,000 would be required to fund the venture, so the business plan would be looking to support a 42,000 investment rather than just 25,000 before stress-testing.

Category	Business Plan		Revenue
			What if
Sales receipts			
Cash sales	50000		50000
Credit sales	50000		50000
Total cash in	100000	Sales the same	100000
Payments			
Salary and wages	25000		35000
Utilities	10000		15000
Rent and rates	15000		12000
Materials	35000		40000
Equipment	40000	Payments increase	40000
Total cash out	125000		142000
Net cash flow	-25000		-42000
Funding needs	-25000	Funding needs +17,000	-42000

Figure 13.2 Testing the payments model

Testing to destruction

Calamitous accidents happen when two relatively unexpected events occur at the same time. For example, on 5 November 2010 a cement lorry fell from Warren Lane Bridge at Oxshott onto the sixth and seventh coaches of an eight-car passenger service, derailing the train, seriously injuring the lorry driver and two passengers and causing days of major traffic disruption. Had the lorry fallen a couple of seconds later it would have missed the train completely.

From a business planning perspective it is more likely that a couple of things will go wrong over the planning horizon than with this type of railway disaster. Using the cashflow model, check out a number of possible problem areas and see at what point these problems would cause you or your financial backers sleepless nights. For example, what would the effect be of a major customer going bust, a supplier putting their prices up and a key employee leaving unexpectedly, all in the same quarter?

Figure 13.3 shows a hypothetical example of how you might test the effects of various events – sales coming in being less than expected and payments out being higher. In this case the net effect calls for a funding requirement of 62,000 rather than the 25,000 originally projected. So if you are unable to lay your hands on an extra 37,000 those are circumstances that would cause your business to run out of cash and in all probability fail.

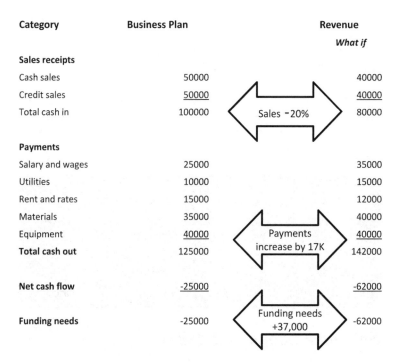

Category	Business Plan		Revenue
			What if
Sales receipts			
Cash sales	50000		40000
Credit sales	50000		40000
Total cash in	100000	Sales −20%	80000
Payments			
Salary and wages	25000		35000
Utilities	10000		15000
Rent and rates	15000		12000
Materials	35000		40000
Equipment	40000	Payments increase by 17K	40000
Total cash out	125000		142000
Net cash flow	-25000		-62000
Funding needs	-25000	Funding needs +37,000	-62000

Figure 13.3 Testing to destruction

Firebox.com's co-creator and founder of Mind Candy, Michael Smith, went through some pretty dark times at Firebox as a lot of dotcom businesses did. When the NASDAQ peaked on 11 March 2000, and then started its precipitous decline, his business followed suit. "We realised we were in a very serious situation," says Smith. "We took stock, looked at the business and realised if we were going to survive we were going to have to make some very drastic changes. We had to lay-off about 20 people. We moved to tiny little offices in Brixton. We stopped taking salaries. We stretched our suppliers as much as we could and felt that if we could just keep trading until Christmas we'd survive. Christmas was about six months away at the time, so it was a really horrible time, lots of sleepless nights and grey hairs. But, by the skin of our teeth, we managed to make it. We turned a £400,000 loss into a £400,000 profit the year after. We are very glad we did keep going despite all the advice we had got to close the business down. For me it's definitely my most valuable lesson as an entrepreneur: I now absolutely understand the value of cash, and preserving it. Even if you raise cash from outside, whether it's a loan or an investment, treat it incredibly carefully, and always watch your costs. All investors have to treat cash the same way, and watch it like a hawk."

The funding needs projected in your business plan should accommodate a realistic amount of revenue shortfall and cost overrun. Realistic is not an easy word to define, but the volatility of your business sector and the prevailing economic climate should be taken into account.

> ### Startups Tip
> Bad cashflow management can be the death of even the busiest and most profitable of businesses, so it's crucial to put the right processes in place to ensure things run smoothly. The Startups webpage on this topic (www.startups.co.uk/cashflow) includes tips on how to make sure your business has good cashflow, and advice on how to get things back on track if you run into tricky financial periods.

Holding a tiger by the tail

Stresses can work in both directions. What if your business plan projections are too conservative? Table 13.3 shows the first four months of trading for a new business. The business plan projected sales growing from 3,000 to 7,000 over the period, but the actual results turned out to be much greater – the word greater here is more appropriate than better. Predictability is valued more highly than nearly anything else when it comes to financial performance.

TABLE 13.3: Overtrading

Month	Apr	May	June	July
Receipts:				
Sales	4,000	5,000	5,000	7,000
Owner's cash	10,000			
Bank loan	10,000			
Total cash in	24,000	5,000	5,000	7,000
Payments:				
Purchases	5,500	2,950	4,220	7,416
Rates, electricity, heat, telephone, internet, etc	1,000	1,000	1,000	1,000
Wages	1,000	1,000	1,000	1,000
Advertising	1,550	1,550	1,550	1,550
Fixtures/fittings	11,550			
Computer, etc	1,000			
Total cash out	21,550	6,550	7,700	10,966
Monthly cash surplus/ (defecit)	2,450	(1,500)	(2,700)	(3,966)
Cumulative cash balance	2,450	950	(1,820)	(5,786)

Based on the business plan, the owner put in 10,000 and raised a 10,000 bank loan, but by month 3 had run out of cash. The build up of sales sounds good, but for much of these orders the cash will not come in for anything up to 12 weeks. In the meantime, wages must be met and a growing army of suppliers paid promptly or materials will dry up. In line with the faster sales growth, stock levels have to be raised or hard won customers will be disappointed when they reorder.

In this example, the business looks like having insufficient cash, based on the assumptions made. An outsider, a banker perhaps, would look at the figures in month 4 and see a business in trouble.

The figures in Table 13.3 indicate a business that is trading beyond its financial resources, a condition known as 'overtrading' – anathema to bankers the world over. You can do a number of 'what if' projections to include with your business plan showing what the cash position will be if a much larger base of customers comes on board, and at what point you will become cashflow positive. If the owner of this business had forewarned their bankers of the consequences of faster sales growth in their business plan, they may well have been able to raise an additional 6,000 of overdraft finance to smooth over the transition to a higher sales plateau.

Measuring milestones

Pitching for funds is always a bit of a balancing act. Ask for too little and you run the danger of overtrading; too much and you scare them off. Having performance milestones built into the business plan is one way of showing investors and bankers what is happening to their money before you become profitable, and under what circumstances you may need more money still (Table 13.4).

Table 13.4 shows how you can set out the milestones so that investors can feel comfortable with how their money is being spent. No one is going to pump in the whole cash sum required to fund your business on day one, so this is an essential part of the process.

Reviewing the possibilities of insuring against risks

Insurance was covered in Chapter 12, but it would be prudent to re-examine the subject in the light of having stress-tested your model.

Table 13.4 Business plan milestones

Date	Milestone	Measure	Cash implications
Month 1	Finalise UK patents	Approval granted	10,000
Month 2	Beta trial prototype	50 customers test and feedback	5,000
Month 3	Launch website	Website trials run, bugs sorted out and in first page of Google	10,000
Month 4	Recruit sales team	Sales manager appointed	10,000
Month 5	Full sales launch	If sales as per business plan	20,000
		If sales above business plan	5,000 per 50,000 sales over plan

Credit insurance

An independent research study of 2,000 businesses in 10 European economies by the Credit Management Research Centre at Leeds University Business School indicated that bad debts represent on average 0.74% for non-insured companies against 0.38% for companies using credit insurance. While that may not sound too dramatic, when you consider that most companies make less than 10% profit, losing 0.36% through lack of insurance (0.74–0.38) is a hefty slice: around 3.6% of potential extra gains.

Credit insurers' business proposition rests simply on the fact that they have better information; the big ones track the performance of over 40 million companies worldwide. Also, they don't have to base their credit decisions on short-term risks solely on the basis of an 18-month-old P&L and balance sheet and a rough credit score. Regional risk offices established in the major cities are in charge of making direct contact with buyers (the clients of their clients) and of obtaining the most up-to-date information on their financial position (see Chapter 14 for more on this subject).

Foreign exchange risk

This type of risk occurs when a business incurs costs or generates revenues in any currency other than the one shown in its filed accounts. Two types of event can lead to an exchange rate risk: a mismatch between cost of sales (manufacturing etc) incurred in one currency and the actual sales income generated in another; and any time lag between setting the selling price in one currency and the date the customer actually pays up. As it is unlikely that there will have been no movement in exchange rates, transaction risk is real and could potentially have serious consequences.

There are a number of options for limiting the dangers of unexpected violent fluctuations, eg buying the currency forward. A forward contract fixes the rate of exchange for a period so guaranteeing that you receive the Sterling value of any sales made in a foreign currency irrespective of market changes.

> ### Startups Tip
>
> Business insurance can be complex for a start-up or new business. The insurance comparison tool on the Startups website will enable you to compare quotes and buy the most appropriate insurance cover for your business (www.startups.co.uk/business-insurance.html).

Checklist

☑ Consider the key assumptions that underpin the projections in your business.

☑ List five factors that could adversely affect your sales projections, and five that could adversely affect your costs and expense projections. What are the implications?

☑ Set out a milestone chart for the key results and costs that will satisfy investors/lenders that their money is being spent wisely.

☑ Identify key risk factors that you could/should insure against.

↪ CHAPTER 14

Planning for change and growth

📖 What's in this chapter?

Nothing lasts forever or indeed for very long in the business world. The fax machine, the must-have device of the late 1980s, was rated as the greatest business communication tool to hit the market in quarter of a century. Less than a decade later it was a commodity product heading for extinction. Your business planning should include procedures for taking account of the changes that are likely to occur in your industry, and what steps you will take to keep your business on a growth trajectory.

In this chapter we'll cover:

→ lifecycle strategies
→ assessing portfolio prospects
→ reviewing growth options
→ franchising
→ raising serious money
→ planning for an exit.

Lifecycle strategies

The idea that business products and services have a lifecycle was first seen in management literature as far back as 1922, when researchers looking at the growth of the US automobile industry observed a bell-shaped pattern for the sales of individual cars. The length of a product's lifetime can be centuries, as with, say, OXO, or just weeks or months in the case of fads such as the hula-hoop or fashion clothing products.

Products and services typically go through five distinct stages over their life from birth to death, or are re-launched if that proves to be a viable marketing strategy.

1. **Research and development:** this stage is typified by cash outlays only and can last decades in the case of medical products or a few months, even weeks, for a simple consumer product.

2. **Introduction:** here the product is brought to market, perhaps just to one initial segment, and it may comprise little more than a test marketing activity. Once again, costs are high; advertising and selling costs have to be borne up front and sales revenues will be minimum.

3. **Growth:** this stage sees the product sold across the whole range of a company's market segments, gaining market acceptance and becoming profitable.

4. **Maturity and saturation:** sales peak as the limit of customers' capacity to consume is reached and competitors or substitute products enter the market. Profit starts to tail off as prices drop and advertising is stepped up to beat off competitors.

5. **Decline:** sales and profits fall away as competition becomes heavy and better and more competitive, or technologically more advanced products come into the market.

The usefulness of the lifecycle as a marketing tool is as an aid to deciding on the appropriate strategy to incorporate into your business plan. For example, at the introduction stage the goal for advertising and promotion may be to inform and educate; during the growth stage differences need to be stressed to keep competitors at bay; during maturity customers need to be reminded you are still around and it is time to buy again. During decline, it is probable that advertising budgets could be cut and prices lowered. As all major costs associated with the product will have been covered at this point this should still be a profitable stage.

Of course, these are only examples of possible strategies rather than rules to be followed. For example, many products are successfully re-launched during the decline stage by changing an element of the marketing mix or by repositioning into a different marketplace. Hindustan Motors, India's oldest motor company, gave Britain's long defunct Morris Oxford a new lease of life. The last Oxford rolled of the production lines in Cowley in 1959 and in substantially the same form is still rolling off the production lines in the Uttarpara factory in West Bengal.

Figure 14.1 shows a hypothetical lifecycle strategy for Marks & Spencer as it extends the life of its brand with new lifecycle initiatives.

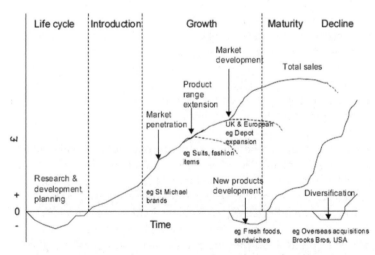

Figure 14.1 Business plan strategies over the product/service lifecycle

> **Startups Tip**
> You can monitor sales of your products and services using spreadsheets such as those provided free at www.jaxworks.com/library.htm.

Assessing your product portfolio

Developed by the Boston Consulting Group (BCG), the American management consultants, the BCG matrix can be used in conjunction with the lifecycle concept (see above and Figure 14.2) to plan a portfolio of product/service offers.

The thinking behind the matrix is that a company's products and services should be classified according to their cash generating or consumption ability against two dimensions: the market growth rate and the company's market share. Cash is used as the measure rather than profit, as that is the real resource used to invest in new offers. The objective then is to use the positive cashflow generated from 'cash cows', usually mature products that no longer need heavy marketing support, to invest in 'stars', that is, fast growing, usually newer products, positioned in markets in which the company already has a high market share – usually newer markets. 'Dogs' should be disinvested and 'question marks' limited in number and watched carefully to see if they are more likely to become stars or dogs. You should show the role, relevant experience and resources that your partners will bring to the venture over the period covered by the business plan, together with their share of the ownership.

Innovation is key to refreshing your product portfolio. Founder of ready meals giant S&A Foods, Perween Warsi, has this to say on the subject: "Innovation is the lifeblood of any company because consumers are becoming more and more discerning; they're always looking for something new, different and exciting. We constantly innovate and launch new products. And we have introduced lots of new concepts as well. The curry pot is a great concept we brought in from America. It took us several attempts to get it right. It's about listening to people."

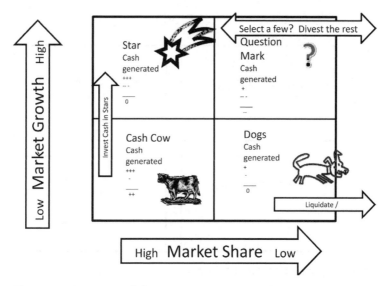

Figure 14.2 BCG matrix

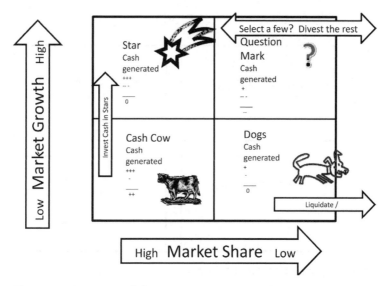

In my experience

Sophie Cornish and Holly Tucker, Notonthehighstreet.com

"We recognise the need to adapt our business model in order to meet the demands of our customers, introducing a printed catalogue to run alongside the online version of the service."

Reviewing growth options

The classic business planning tool for reviewing growth options is Ansoff's growth matrix (see Figure 14.3 over the page), named after the father of strategic planning, Professor Igor Ansoff. Ansoff suggested managers consider growth options as a square matrix divided into four segments. The x-axis is divided into existing and new products, and the

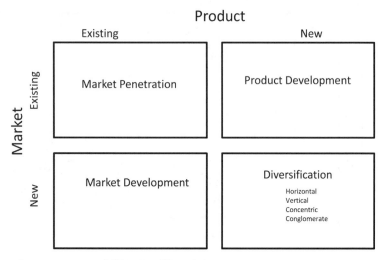

Figure 14.3 Ansoff's growth matrix

y-axis into existing and new markets. Ansoff assigned titles and level of risk to the resulting types of strategies.

⇢ **Market penetration:** this involves selling more of your existing products and services to existing customers; it is the lowest-risk strategy.

⇢ **Product/service development:** involves creating extensions to your existing products, or new products to sell to your existing customer base. This is more risky than market penetration, but less risky than market development.

  ⇢ **Depth of line:** this is the situation when a company has many products within a particular category. Washing powders and breakfast cereals are classic examples of businesses that offer scores of products into the same marketplace. The benefits to the company include that the same channels of distribution and buyers are being used. A weakness is that all these products are subject to similar threats and dangers. However 'deep' your beers and spirits range, for example, you will always face the threat of higher taxes or the opprobrium of those who think you are damaging people's health.

→ **Breadth of line:** this is where a company has a variety of products of different types, such as Marlboro with cigarettes and fashion clothing, or 3M with its extensive variety of adhesives and adhesive-related products, such as Post-it® notes.

→ **Market development:** involves entering new market segments or completely new markets, either in your home country or abroad. You will face new competitors and may not understand the customers as well as you do your current ones.

→ **Diversification:** is selling new products into new markets: the most risky strategy as both are relative unknowns. Avoid this strategy unless all others have been exhausted. Diversification can be further subdivided into four categories of increasing risk profile:

→ **Horizontal diversification:** entirely new product into current market.

→ **Vertical diversification:** move backwards into company's suppliers or forward into customer's business.

→ **Concentric diversification:** new product closely related to current products either in terms of technology or marketing presence but in a new market.

→ **Conglomerate diversification:** completely new product into a new market.

> ### Startups Tip
> Selling into overseas markets can be a great way of winning new customers, broadening your profile and picking up valuable, transferable business skills. See the Startups section on this topic (www.startups.co.uk/selling-abroad).

Use Ansoff's growth matrix to check that your business plan contains a reasonable balance of strategies. Too much emphasis on achieving growth, say through diversification or launching new products, may seem too risky to new sources of finance.

In my experience

Mary and Doug Perkins, Specsavers

"We have continued to lead by innovation and drive the company forward by continually investing in state-of-the-art eye equipment, product innovation, staff training and consumer satisfaction research. We diversified into hearing centres in 2002, and in 2008 a new website enabled customers to buy online. Specsavers is also now the largest provider of home-delivery contact lenses in Europe."

Franchising

Franchising is one growth strategy that answers three important business planning questions: Is there a market? Who will put up most of the money? Who will manage the new operations? Franchising operates in hundreds of business sectors, providing both service – such as advertising, accounting and web design – as well as products. A PricewaterhouseCoopers study shows that in the developed economies there are more than one million franchised establishments producing one out of every seven jobs.

The franchisor supplies the product or teaches the service to the franchisee, who in turn sells it to the public. In return for this, the franchisee pays a fee and a continuing royalty, based usually on turnover. They may also be required to buy materials or ingredients from the franchisor, giving them an additional income stream. The advantage to the franchisee is a relatively safe and quick way of getting into business for themselves, but with the support and advice of an experienced organisation close at hand.

The franchisor can expand their distribution with the minimum strain on their own capital and have the services of a highly motivated team of owner-managers.

> **Startups Tip**
> Check out to see if any other businesses in your sector are using the franchising model to grow. You can find out all about franchising at Startups (www.startups.co.uk/start-a-franchise).

Forging strategic alliances

The most successful businesses forge relationships with businesses up and down their supply chain that go beyond simply buying and selling. Unity Group chairman and serial start-up entrepreneur, Jeremy Harbour, is an advocate here: "When I've looked at businesses I quite often find that if you look at all of the products and services you supply, and all of the customers you've got, your product penetration into those customers is normally about 10% or 15%. So, if you're doing £1 million turnover, there's potentially another £9 million worth of sales that are already in that customer base that you're just not accessing. And if it's a question there not being that much potential in there, then perhaps you need to look at adding some new products. So partner with someone who wants to target your customer base and white label their products with your brand and sell them into your customer base because there's some really quick wins available."

> **Startups Tip**
> Visit Startups (www.startups.co.uk/buy-a-business) to get better informed about the process of buying a business, from company valuation to carrying out due diligence.

More formal relationships that can be incorporated into a business plan for growth include the following over the page.

-> **Acquisitions:** when one company buys another – more often than not in a 'friendly' deal, but sometimes events are not so harmonious. After the acquisition only the parent company usually exists in any real legal sense and the top management of the 'victim' usually depart quickly.

-> **Mergers:** where companies join forces and the separate identities of the businesses of the companies concerned continue after the deal is consummated.

-> **Joint ventures:** when two or more companies decide to set up a separate third business to exploit something together. There may be no attempt to harmonise the whole of the two parent businesses, and the joint venture may be disbanded when the reasons they joined forces in the first place disappear.

In my experience

Edwina Dunn and Clive Humby, dunnhumby

"In 2003, we formed a 50:50 joint venture with Kroger, the largest grocer in the USA, calling the venture dunnhumby USA. We were tasked with transforming the grocer's customer initiatives using its Frequent Shopper Card, and to improve price, assortment and promotions. This is a model we have successfully repeated elsewhere. In October 2006, we created dunnhumby France with Groupe Casino, the French grocery retailer, helping to build on their loyalty and customer first programme."

Managing change

The story most frequently told to illustrate the dangers of ignoring the need for change is that of the hypothetical frog dropped into a pot of boiling water. The immediate impact of a radically different environment spurs the frog into action, leaping out of the pot. The same frog placed in the same pot, where the initial temperature is much lower, will happily allow itself to be boiled to death, failing to recognise the danger if the process is slow enough.

The first task of a leader, therefore, is to define an organisation's purpose and direction. This inevitably means changing these in response to changing circumstances. The business plan should show how such changes will be managed and the new goals achieved.

Because change is inevitable and unpredictable in its consequences doesn't mean that it can't be managed as a process and incorporated into your business plan. These are the stages in managing change:

→ **Tell people why:** change is better accepted when people are given a compelling business reason. Few bankers would question the need for change after the 2008 debacles at Bear Stearns, SocGen and Northern Rock.

→ **Make it manageable:** even when people accept what needs to be done, the change may just be too big for anyone to handle. Breaking it down into manageable chunks can help overcome this.

→ **Take a shared approach:** involve people early, asking them to join you in managing change. Give key participants some say in shaping the change right from the start; this will reduce the feeling that change is being imposed and more brains will be brought to bear on the problem.

→ **Reward success early:** flag up successes as quickly as possible. Don't wait for the year-end or the appraisal cycle. This will inspire confidence and keep the change process on track.

→ **Expect resistance:** not everyone will be equally enthusiastic or committed to change. Some people may lose status, power or even pay. The trick here is to lever on the people who will help, recognise those who could hinder and plan accordingly.

→ **Recognise that change takes longer than expected:** people typically go through seven stages when experiencing change – immobilisation or shock; disbelief; depression; acceptance of reality; testing out the new situation; rationalising why it's happening; and then, finally, acceptance. Most major changes make things worse before they make them better. More often than not the immediate impact of change is a decrease in productivity as people struggle to cope with new ways of working, while they move up their own learning curve. The doubters will gloat and even the change champions may waver, but the greatest danger now is pulling the plug on the plan and either adopting a new plan or reverting to the status quo. To prevent this 'disappointment', it is vital to both set realistic goals for the change period and to anticipate the time lag between change and results.

Raising serious money

Silicon Valley entrepreneur and founder of virtual world Second Life, Philip Rosedale, took several years to move up the 'ladder of finance': "In 1999, Second Life was such an 'out there' idea it didn't seem likely we would be able to raise venture capital investment on day one, so I invested in the company for the first year and a half out of my own pocket. We were six people when we did our first external investment. That investment was in March 2001, so it had been close to a couple of years. The first investments in the company externally came from angel investors and a very small venture capital firm. And so we did that, and I think this is reasonable for lots of new businesses. We went from self-investment to angel investment after a couple of years and then our first big venture capital investment didn't come until 2004, quite a bit later."

If you are aiming for significant growth, you will need a business plan that reflects the needs of those who provide large amounts of capital. Stock markets are the place where serious businesses raise serious money. It's possible to raise anything from a few million to tens of billions; expect the costs and efforts in getting listed to match those stellar figures. The basic idea is that owners sell shares in their businesses that in effect brings in a whole raft of new 'owners' who in turn have a stake in the business's future profits. When they want out, they sell their shares on to other investors. The share price moves up and down to ensure that there are as many buyers as sellers at any one time.

Going public also puts a stamp of respectability on you and your company. It will enhance the status and credibility of your business, and it will enable you to borrow more against the 'security' provided by your new shareholders, should you so wish. Your shares will also provide an attractive way to retain and motivate key staff. If they are given, or rather are allowed to earn, share options at discounted prices, they too can participate in the capital gains you are making.

Initial Public Offer (IPO): criteria for getting a stock market listing

The rules vary from market to market but below are the conditions that are likely to apply to get a company listed on an exchange and which must be incorporated into your business plan. Your business plan should also show the timetable for the final months during the run up to the float, as this process is known.

Financial track record

Getting listed on a major stock exchange calls for a track record of making substantial profits with decent seven figure sums being made in the year you plan to float. The objective is to have a profit record which is rising in a reasonably controlled manner rather than meteoric bursts of growth followed by slumps. Your accounts must have been audited to appropriate accounting standards and the audit reports must not contain any major qualifications.

Advisors

You will need to be supported by a team which will include a sponsor, stockbroker, reporting accountant and solicitor. These professionals will expect your business plan to be prepared to a high standard. Advisors should be respected firms, active in flotation work and familiar with the company's type of business. You and your business may be judged by the company you keep, so choose advisors of good repute and make sure that the personalities work effectively together. It is very unlikely that a small local firm of accountants, however satisfactory, will be up to this task.

Management team

The company's directors and senior staff will be fully occupied in providing information and attending meetings over the period leading up to the float. They will have to delegate operating tasks that they might otherwise have been responsible for, so your business plan should show that there is sufficient depth of management to ensure that the business does not suffer.

Non-executive directors

Sometimes a heavyweight outsider can lend extra credibility to an ambitious business plan. If you know or have access to someone with a successful track record in your area of business you should invite them to help. Non-executive directors do need to have relevant experience or be able to open doors and do deals. Check out organisations such as Venture Investment Partners (www.ventureip.co.uk) and the Independent Director Initiative (www.independentdirector.co.uk), a joint venture between Ernst & Young and the Institute of Directors, for information on tracking down the right non-executive director for your business.

In my experience

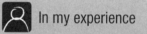

Edwina Dunn and Clive Humby, dunnhumby

"We built our reputation on the strength of our work for Tesco so it wasn't surprising that in the heady days when the dotcom boom was in full swing we were approached several times to float the company. Some valuations reached £1 billion. We could not quite believe such valuations were possible so we declined to float. Instead we took an offer from Tesco to buy a 53% stake in the business."

Planning for an exit

If your business plan is intended to help you sell the business and move on you need to make the business look its best. Blemishes such as poor profit performance, bad debts, credit downgrades, and being dragged through the courts by ex-employees claiming to have been unfairly dismissed, are not desirable. You should try to make the three years prior to your exit look as good as possible. That means profit margins should be consistently high, the sales and profit curve should be heading upwards, and strong financial control systems should be in evidence. Your business plan should also show that the business has scope for improvement and development if someone with more money and wider skills and experience takes it forward. Otherwise it's hard for a potential buyers to see what value they can add.

Startups Tip

Creditgate.com (www.creditgate.com) and Credit Reporting (www.creditreporting.co.uk/b2b) offer a comprehensive range of credit reports instantly online, including credit check, credit rating, company profile, credit score, credit reference, credit limit, company directors, and CCJs. You can get your own business rating from one of these agencies to see how you appear to a would-be buyer.

The Centre for Inter-firm Comparison (www.cifc.co.uk) helps businesses of every kind improve their profitability and productivity by providing expertise in benchmarking, performance measurement and financial control. It gathers financial information on industries based on detailed information that participating businesses provide (in absolute confidence) on a comparable basis. The information is then provided showing industry average and best and worst performance standards, without, of course, revealing the individual participants' data.

In my experience

Edwina Dunn and Clive Humby, dunnhumby

"In 2006, Tesco increased its stake in the business from 53% to 84% and in January 2011 they bought the remaining 16%, leaving us free to exit the business."

Checklist

☑ Position your products on the BCG matrix and consider which dogs to ditch, cows to milk, question marks to grow and stars to shine with.

☑ Using Ansoff's growth matrix, list the options to grow your business over the period of your business plan, ranking them in order of preference.

☑ Consider whether you could form any strategic alliances or joint ventures, with whom and to what effect.

☑ Consider what options are available for raising serious money, and so being able to propel your business to the next level.

☑ Identify your exit strategy.

↻ *CHAPTER 15*

Writing, presenting and refining your business plan

📖 What's in this chapter?

The preceding chapters have been about the all-important data assembly and its subsequent analysis and interpretation – the foundations of every sound business plan. Now this information has to be assembled, collated and orchestrated into a coherent and complete written business plan aimed at and presented to a specific audience. Think of the earlier chapters as substance and this one as being all about style. Even a great business strategy can be further enhanced by a powerful, visually pleasing and accurate written document.

In this chapter we'll cover:

→ dividing up the task
→ matching your words to your readers
→ creating a great impression
→ using business planning software
→ revising the plan
→ preparing for the oral presentation
→ refining your business plan.

Dividing up the task

The preceding chapters have identified manageable 'chunks' of material to write up, either yourself or (better still) to delegate to partners and professional advisors.

While it is useful to make use of as much help as you can get in preparing the groundwork, you should orchestrate the information and write the business plan yourself. After all, it is your future that is at stake – and every prospective financier will be backing you and your ability to put this plan into action, not your scriptwriter.

Different people in your team will have been responsible for carrying out the work involved in actioning the checklists that have been provided at the end of each chapter in this book and in writing up different section(s) of the business plan. This information should be circulated to ensure that:

→ everyone is still heading in the same direction. Inevitably, thinking will change as a result of discussion and debate. For example, the cashflow stress tests may cause significant alterations to an original strategy;

→ nothing important has been missed out. Two or more sets of eyes are always better at spotting any gaps. Also, as the business plans originator and champion, you will be close to the subject and as such are in danger of taking for granted how much an outside reader really knows and understands.

Establish a timetable for when each section of the business plan should be ready in draft form, showing who is responsible for each task and when it should be completed (see Table 15.1).

TABLE 15.1 Business plan collaborative writing milestone

Business area	Task	Person responsible	Date for completion	Confirm completion
Marketing	Confirm media to be used and costs	Bill	1 March	
Human Resources	Recommend staff recruitment strategy, cost and timing	Sara	15 March	
Accounting and finance	Prepare cashflow forecasts and the 'what if' cashflow template	Tim	15 April	

Startups Tip

Use a group writing tool such as the track changes facility in Microsoft Word. In that way everyone involved can see who said or changed what and when changes were made.

Matching your words to your readers

A business plan is a professional document, and though its primary purpose is to 'sell' your proposition to someone, it is not a sales advertisement. Try to bear in mind the following points.

-> Keep your sentences short. Twenty words or so is about right, while above 30 makes it harder to keep track of the sense of the sentence.

-> Use short simple words where they mean much the same, for example 'fast' not 'expeditious'.

-> Avoid jargon, and if you have to use technical words keep them to a minimum and supply a glossary rather than explain their meaning in the body of the text.

↠ Use headings to break up your text. These will act as signposts so your reader can see where they are and what lies ahead.

↠ Use active section headings, 'Large growing market, few established competitors', for example, when you want to prepare your reader for important information that underpins your arguments.

↠ Use passive section headings such as 'Introduction', 'Cashflow forecast', 'Management team' when you just want the reader to know where they are in your business plan.

↠ Strike a balance between a formal and more active writing style. This can be difficult to master, but what matters more is consistency. Though your plan may take months to get together, and be written by several people, it has to read as one document, with a consistent writing style.

↠ Keep the document short. There are no hard and fast rules about how long a business plan should be, but 50 pages or more will raise a groan as your reader picks it up. You need to strike a balance between completeness and impact. Your reader will be able to ask questions later if they want to know more about a certain aspect of your business proposition. It takes longer to write a concise business plan. George Bernard Shaw's line at the end of a long letter to a friend "If I had more time I would have sent you a postcard", certainly applies here.

> ### Startups Tip
> Texas University (http://writingcenter.tamu.edu/how-to/business) has a number of valuable teaching notes on business writing, covering sentence and paragraph construction, the use of words and on 'beginning the writing process: brainstorming, researching and outlining'.

Inevitably a business plan is aimed at a number of different audiences who have diverse if overlapping requirements. Clearly, much of the contents of the business plan will be common to all these audiences. Your core proposition, the target markets, business strategy, operating procedures will be of importance to all your readers. But the order of content, the amount of information and some of the words used may on some occasions be used differently for each key reader group to have the best chance of achieving your goal in writing the business plan.

Investors will be most interested in hearing about exciting future prospects, bankers will be looking for evidence of a sound foundation while a prospective key employee will hope for evidence of career opportunities. If the plan is to be pitched at a corporate venture fund (see Chapter 11) they will want strong evidence of valuable intellectual property (see Chapter 6) or some other attribute that they can leverage into their own business at some point.

You may also find it useful to produce a rolling business plan to include modifications in the light of events as they develop. A successful pitch to a business angel confirming commitment in principle to provide funds could be incorporated into later editions of your business plan as a material fact. The results from customer trials not available when your business plan was written first can be added as they become available.

Making your writing readable

Many business plans are difficult to read. Two things make life hard for readers: long sentences and long words. Back in 1952, Robert Gunning, a business language expert, devised a formula to measure just how tough a memo, letter, or report is to read, called the Fog Index.

The Fog Index

1. Find the average number of words per sentence. Use a sample at least 100 words long. Divide the total number of words by the number of sentences to give you the average sentence length.
2. Count the number of words of three syllables or more per 100 words. Don't count (a) words that are capitalised; (b) combinations of short easy words like 'bookkeeper'; (c) verbs that are made up of three syllables by adding 'ed' or 'es' like 'created' or 'trespasses'.

3. Add the two factors above and multiply by 0.4. This will give you the Fog Index. It corresponds roughly with the number of years of schooling a person would require to read a passage with ease and understanding.

4. Check the results against this scale:
   - 4 and below: very easy, perhaps childish
   - 5 fairly easy: tabloid press, hard-selling letters
   - 7 or 8 standard: *Daily Mail*, most business letters
   - 9–11 fairly difficult: *The Times*, *The Daily Telegraph*, good product literature
   - 12–15 difficult: *The Economist*, technical literature
   - 17 or above very difficult: *New Scientist* – don't use in business plans.

You can find a neat tool at this weblink (www.gunning-fog-index.com/). Just copy and paste the text you want checked into the box and the Fog Index is calculated for you.

Creating a great impression

Your business plan should be visually appealing. Dense text, poor layout and clutter all serve to put your reader off. Create a favourable impression from the outset and you will have them onside. These are the most important guidelines to make your written business plan stand out from the crowd.

→ **Layout:** the reasoning behind good layout is to entice the reader to read your words and take the action you want – back your proposition. Give your text room to breathe by leaving plenty of white space around it. You can achieve this by having wide margins. Use headlines to break up the text and different font sizes and styles to differentiate between sections of your business plan.

→ **Font:** don't be tempted to use a fancy font in the body of the business plan. Stick to serif fonts (those with slight 'tails' on the letters) that lead the eye from letter to letter. Times Roman, Book Antiqua and Century are good examples of texts that cause less eye-strain. Sans-serif fonts – Arial, Calibri and Helvetica for example – can cause eye-fatigue when used in text so are best used in headlines, bullets or short paragraphs outside of the main body. Never use a font smaller than 10 point, unless your readership is mostly under 30. Most business plan writers settle on 12 point as the preferred size.

↝ **Pictures:** images, charts, tables, graphs and pictures are powerful ways to convey large amounts of information quickly and efficiently. A picture, so the saying goes, is worth a thousand words, which is excellent as they usually only need the space of 200! This is also a great way to break up the text and retain reader attention.

> ### Startups Tip
> Check out Startups guide to presentation software (www.startups.co.uk/what-is-presentation-software.html) where you can find out how Microsoft PowerPoint, Harvard Graphics, Impress and Lotus Freelance Graphics can help you put together a professional business plan presentation using charts, graphs, charts, pictures and more.

Using business planning software

You may consider taking some of the sweat out of writing your business plan by using one of the myriad software programmes on the market. You need to take some care in using such systems because the result can be a bland plan that pleases no one and achieves nothing worthwhile.

Don't buy a package with several hundred business plans covering every type of business imaginable. The chances are that the person who wrote the plans knows far less than you do about your business sector and can add little or no value to your proposition. Worse still, at least an even chance exists that the reader of your plan has seen the fruits of these packaged plans before and may be less than enthusiastic to see yet another one.

Good business planning software provides a useful structure to drop your plan into, and may provide a few helpful spreadsheets and templates for financial projections and market analysis. It also provides a valuable repository for your work in progress as you assemble the evidence to convince yourself and others that your business can succeed.

What software does not do is write a convincing business proposition by itself. The maxim 'garbage in garbage out' applies to business planning software just as it does to everything to do with computers. The other danger is that you end up with spreadsheet solutions and numbers just pumped into the financials and without any evidence of the underlying logic to support them.

> **Startups Tip**
> Use business planning software as an aid and not a crutch. Go beyond that and you may end up worse off than if you had started with a blank sheet of paper.

Check out on Startups (www.startups.co.uk/business-plan-calculators) for tools to help you put together your business plan.

Revising your draft

When you have finished assembling the various sections of your business plan, and writing what you can think of as a first draft, it is always prudent to get some final feedback before going live. A 'prospectus', such as a business plan seeking finance from investors, can have a legal status, turning any claims you may make for sales and profits (for example) into a 'contract'. Your accountant and legal advisor will be able to help you with the appropriate language that can convey your projections without giving them contractual status. This would also be a good time to talk over the proposal with a 'friendly' banker or venture capital provider. They can give an insider's view as to the strengths and weaknesses of your proposal.

However much help you get with writing your business plan it is still just that – your plan. So, the responsibility for the final proof-reading before it goes out must rest with you. Spelling mistakes and typing errors can have a disproportionate influence on the way your business plan is received. Venture capitalists and bankers tend to think that if you are careless with your words you could be equally cavalier with their cash.

Protecting your plan

Before you show or discuss your business plan with anyone outside of your organisation you should consider getting them to sign a non-disclosure agreement (NDA). NDAs are confidentiality agreements that bind recipients to maintain your 'secrets' and not to take any action that could damage the value of any 'secret'. This means that they can't share the information with anyone else or act on the idea themselves, for a period of time at least. NDAs are a helpful way of getting advice and help while protecting you from someone using your information to compete against you.

Doing the final edit

Once your first draft has been revised comes the task of editing. Here the grammar, spelling and language must be carefully checked to ensure that your business plan is concise, correct, clear and complete – and not too long. If writing is not your trade, once again this is an area in which to seek help. Your local college or librarian will know of someone who can produce 'attention-capturing' prose, if you yourself don't.

The other purpose of editing is to reduce the business plan to between 20 and 40 pages. However complex or sizeable the venture, outsiders won't have time to read it if it is longer, and insiders will only succeed in displaying their muddled thinking to full effect.

A degree of prudence is a virtue the business plan writer should cultivate. One way to improve the quality of your writing is, once you have a near final draft, to put it aside until the next morning. Research conducted by scientists at the Surrey Sleep Research Centre at the University of Surrey has found that sleeping on a problem really can help solve it. They tested whether 'incubating' a problem allowed a flash of insight, and found it did. A similar study at the University of California San Diego showed that sleep improved creative problem-solving ability by almost 40%.

Preparing for the oral presentation

If getting someone interested in your business plan is half the battle in raising funds, the other half is the oral presentation. Researchers have shown that each of the following elements has a value in transmitting a message:

→ words: 7%

→ tone: 35%

→ non-verbal or body language: 58%.

You may disagree with these percentages, but think about it for a moment. You have complete control over the words that you use but you have less control over the tone of your speech so you must work hard to sound professional, interested, open to criticism and friendly without being over familiar. You have limited control over your non-verbal signals, your body language. Subconsciously your body will reveal what you really mean and think.

If you sit with your arms and legs crossed, this is a defensive posture and indicates a hostile attitude towards the other person and/or the message. Sitting with your arms folded with your thumbs up, shows a superior attitude. Leaning forward indicates either interest or intimidation. People who rest their chin on one hand and have a finger in or near their mouth need reassurance. Those who rub their chins are thinking or making a decision and will not be listening to you.

Gestures are intentional movements and should not be confused with body language.

You may be able to control your body language at the beginning of a conversation, but the more you become involved, the more your subconscious will take over.

Body language at the beginning of a conversation is absolutely key to a successful presentation. Of information relayed, 87% comes from the eyes, 9% the ears, and 4% is via the other senses (taste, touch and smell).

Any organisation financing a venture will insist on seeing the team involved presenting and defending its plans – in person. They know that they are backing people every bit as much as the idea. You can be sure that any financiers you are presenting to will be well prepared. Remember that they see hundreds of proposals every year, and either have (or know of) investments in many different sectors of the economy. If this is not your first business venture, they may even have taken the trouble to find out something of your past financial history.

Founding father of European venture capital Sir Ronald Cohen states: "The biggest mistake entrepreneurs who come pitching for capital make is that they deliver the pitch they've prepared instead of trying to find out what it is the person sitting on the other side of the table with the money is really concerned about. You find entrepreneurs going on for 25 or 30 minutes without giving anybody a chance to breathe, instead of asking 'Could you tell me what concerns you about my business plan?'"

Keep these points in mind when preparing for the presentation of your business plan.

→ Find out how much time you have then rehearse your presentation beforehand. Allow at least as much time for questions as for your talk.

→ Use visual aids and, if possible, bring and demonstrate your product or service. A video, computer-generated model or diagram can help bring your proposition to life.

→ Explain your strategy in a business-like manner, demonstrating your grasp of the competitive market forces at work. Listen to comments and criticisms carefully, avoiding a defensive attitude when you respond.

→ Provide the latest information on sales, profits, product development, market tests or other evidence-based milestones. This may be too current to include in your written plan so here is the opportunity to add strength to your proposition.

↦ Make your replies to questions brief and to the point. If members of the audience want more information, they can ask. This approach allows time for the many different questions that must be asked, either now or later, before an investment can proceed.

↦ Your goal is to create empathy between yourself and your listeners. While you may not be able to change your personality, you could take a few tips on presentation skills. Eye contact, tone of speech, enthusiasm and body language all have a part to play in making a presentation successful.

↦ Wearing formal clothing is never likely to upset anyone. Shorts and sandals could just set the wrong tone! Serious money calls for serious people.

↦ Be prepared. You need to have every aspect of your business plan in your head and know your way around the plan forwards, backwards and sideways!

↦ You never know when the chance to present may occur. It's as well to have a 5-, 10- and 20-minute presentation ready to run at a moment's notice. Known as the 'elevator pitch', ie the time it takes to move from the lobby to an office floor in an elevator, this can also be a useful preparation for writing up your executive summary.

> ### Startups Tip
> It's pointless having a great plan if you can't deliver it. Check out the Startups section on this topic to see how you can apply the final touch (www.startups.co.uk/checking-and-pitching-the-plan.html).
>
> You can also check out Startups guide to using presentation software (www.startups.co.uk/tips-for-using-presentation-software.html), where you can find out how to make your business plan presentation keep your audience's attention throughout.

Founder of Ariadne Capital and Online *Dragons' Den* investor, Julie Meyer, offers this advice on what makes a great funding pitch: "The pitch has to get across really quickly what the company does. So for Skype it was 'free calls on the web'. If it has to be explained, or it's too complicated, you lose people pretty quickly. So I think clarity and simplicity of message is really important in a pitch for funding. And the entrepreneur has to strike the right balance between being serious and showing the intent they have and yet showing a human quality; a little bit of fun. The investor is thinking 'Would I work with that person well or would they be a royal pain in the neck?' So the first bit of the pitch is trying to get the investor to fall in love with the proposition, but you're charming the pants off of them, so all of the usual tools of seduction apply."

In my experience

Mary and Doug Perkins, Specsavers

Mary's business plan was aimed at getting opticians to buy into their vision. "We had to get through our first year successfully so we had some satisfactory figures to show other opticians so they would join the group," she recalls.

Refining your business plan

Don't be either surprised or disheartened if your business plan doesn't get the reception you hope for. Anita Roddick's Body Shop proposition was turned down flat. It was only when a local garage owner, Ian McGlinn, advanced her £4,000 in return for 25% of her company that she got the money to open a second shop; a deal that netted him a couple of hundred million and her considerably more. Tim Waterstone's business plan was turned down by bank after bank, for being too ambitious. They wanted him to open a bookshop but he had set his sights on a chain. Eventually he got backing and went on to build his chain, change the shape of book retailing in the UK and selling his business to his former employer, WH Smith, for £47 million.

There are hundreds of reasons why business plans are turned down. According to venture capitalists, who turn down 95 propositions for every 100 they receive, it's just that they are not convinced by the proposition, that the plan has been well thought through, properly researched and that the person or team are up to the task.

The following measures will help you to refine your business plan and minimise the chances of ultimate rejection.

- ⇢ Listen carefully to criticisms when you are presenting your business plan. If it is clear at the time that you are going to be turned down, ask two questions: why; and what can you do to improve your proposition.

- ⇢ Go back over your business plan and see if there is anything you can change to make the financial proposition look less risky. High burn rate, that is cash pouring out in the early weeks and months on staff, offices and PR without any significant sales revenue coming in, is a big turn off for financiers.

- ⇢ If your credibility is questioned it may be time to consider strengthening your team, taking in a non-executive director or building a strategic alliance with an organisation that can plug the gap in question.

- ⇢ Consider whether you are pitching your proposition to the right audience. Risky technology based ventures are more likely to appeal to venture capitalists and corporate venture firms. Bankers are more interested in putting up cash for tangible assets such as property and elements of working capital including stock in trade and financing quality customers taking credit.

- ⇢ If your business proposition is challenged, get out and secure some initial business. If that is impossible get some customers to agree to try out your product, perhaps agreeing to be a trial or demonstration site in return for a reduced price. You can then build in their acceptance as proof that your ideas have potential.

⇥ See if there are elements of cost that can be eliminated, reduced or postponed. For example, a state of art website may be desirable, but a more basic site at a much reduced cost may be enough for the first few weeks and months.

⇥ Is there a radically different approach to delivering your product that could work as a bridge between where you are and where you want to be? For example, one entrepreneur who wanted to open a bagel shop started out with a stall in a street market. Once that was a proven success he went on to launch his shops.

Checklist

☑ Make a checklist of the information still required for your business plan.

☑ If you are working with others, consider dividing the writing task and map out who is going to write what and by when.

☑ List the different audiences for your business plan — banks, venture capital firms, business angels, prospective partners, landlords or key staff — then consider what should be strengthened or reduced in terms of content for each.

☑ Consider what visual materials — graphs, charts, pictures, etc — you can incorporate into your business plan.

☑ Think about what you can do to strengthen your proposition; reduce the costs; speed up the time to break-even; or find a more receptive audience.

CHAPTER 16

The business plan: key elements, structure and contents

What's in this chapter?

This chapter is in effect the culmination of your work to date. Inevitably, everything you have been preparing should be seen as 'work in progress'. At each stage you may well have had to go back and review an earlier one. Now, however, all the strands of the business plan need to be pulled together into a coherent whole. Not every topic will be relevant to every type of business, but the general format should be followed, with emphasis laid as appropriate.

In this chapter we'll cover:

→ packaging your business plan

→ laying out a cover sheet

→ preparing a table of contents

→ using a glossary of terms

→ pulling together an executive summary

→ setting out the body of the business plan

→ employing appendices.

Packaging your business plan

Most products are enhanced by appropriate packaging, and a business plan is no exception. Most business plan readers prefer a simple spiral binding with a plastic cover on the front and back (see Figure 16.1). This makes it easy for the reader to move from section to section, and it ensures the plan will survive frequent handling. Stapled copies and leather-bound tomes are viewed as undesirable extremes.

• Difficult to navigate	• Easy to find your way around
• Frequent handling can loosen pages	• Can survive being passed from reader to reader

Figure 16.1 Packaging your business plan

Laying out a cover sheet

The cover sheet includes your venture's full legal name, address, phone and fax numbers, website, and name and title of the person to contact and their email and phone contact information (Figure 16.2). Also state who the business plan is going to.

While you may well be sending your plan out to several organisations, and those may be identical, it is always helpful to make them feel that the plan is addressed personally to them. Ideally, place each piece of information on a separate line and centre it in the middle of your cover page using a large font. Include your logo, strapline or an image that you use to convey what you do.

Business Plan
For First Travel Adventures Limited

"Travel with first and never look back"
Submitted To Global Venture Providers Inc
Prepared and submitted by:
Mike Godfrey
Managing Director and Founder
First Travel Adventures Ltd
123 Main Street, Newville
MN43 7HH
Company Tel: 00119988
Company Fax: 00 119987
Personal Mobile: 0765 000000
Email: m_godfrey@snl.com
Website: WWW.FTG.Com

Business Plan V.1; 25 January, 2012

Information restricted and provided in confidence

Figure 16.2 An example cover sheet

Lower down the page, put the date of the business plan and its version number; this is important as people receiving your plan could be working from an earlier version if the approval process is drawn out, as is almost inevitable if you are raising venture capital. Include some information showing that the information is provided in confidence, whether or not you require a confidentiality agreement. It will at least put people on their guard before passing on or discussing any aspect of your business plan.

If you are not going to use a full NDA, you should always put a basic NDA in behind the cover sheet (Figure 16.3). This shows the reader that this is a valuable document that you have put considerable thought into.

NON-DISCLOSURE AGREEMENT

I _____ of

_____

hereby undertake as follows

1)   Recognising that certain information in this business plan is supplied in confidence I shall keep as confidential all information disclosed to me by _____ ("the Principal") relating to this business plan whatsoever, without the permission of the Principal, or of an authorised agent.

2)   The undertakings under Clause 1 shall not apply to:

   (i)   any information which I am able to reasonably establish as previously known to me; or

   (ii)   any information provided to me by a third party who has the right to make such information available; or

   (iii) any information which may become public knowledge other than through breach of any undertaking contained herein.

3)   The confidentiality obligation will survive until such time as I may receive formal notice from the Principal, or its authorised agent thereof, of a release therefrom.

Signed: _____

Name: _____

Date: _____

Figure 16.3 An example basic NDA

Preparing a table of contents

A table of contents is the map that will guide the new reader through your business plan and on to the 'inevitable' conclusion that they should back your venture. If a map is obscure, muddled or even missing, then the chances are you will end up with lost or irritated readers unable to find their way around your proposal. Each of the main sections of the business plan should be listed and the pages within that section indicated.

There are two valid schools of thought on page numbering. One favours a straightforward sequential numbering of each page – 1, 2, 3. . . 9, 10 for example. This is perfectly adequate for short, simple plans, dealing with uncomplicated issues and seeking modest levels of finance. Also, most business plans are easier to follow when numbered by section.

Table 16.1 shows how this method works. The section headed 'The business and its management' is section 1, and the pages that follow are listed from 1.1 to 1.7 in the table of contents, so identifying each page as belonging within that specific section. This numbering method also allows you to insert new material without upsetting the entire pagination during preparation. Tables and figures should also be similarly numbered.

TABLE 16.1: Structure of a table of contents

Individual paragraph numbering, much in favour with government and civil service departments, is considered something of overkill in a business plan and is to be discouraged, except perhaps if you are looking for a large amount of government grant.

Using a glossary of terms

A glossary is a list of difficult or unusual words and expressions used in the business plan with accompanying definitions that the lay reader may not understand. It is usually inserted at the top of the table of contents so that readers are forewarned of what is to come. The content of the glossary depends to some extent on who your business plan is aimed at. A venture capital firm specialising in pharmaceuticals, or a company in the sector looking for a corporate venture investment, can reasonably be expected to have a sound grasp of most of the relevant vocabulary. A bank manager, on the other hand, may not.

Example glossary for an internet advertising revenue stream

CPC – cost per click (CPC): An online payment model where advertisers pay for each click through made on their advertisement

CPM – cost per thousand (CPM): An online payment model where advertisers pay for every 1,000 impressions of their advertisement. The 'M' in CPM is from the Roman numeral for 1,000, derived from the Latin word 'mille' meaning 'thousand'.

Click Through Rate: The percentage of impressions that resulted in a click through as calculated by dividing the number of clicks by the number of impressions. For example, if a banner was clicked on 15 times after being displayed 1,000 times, the banner would have a click rate of $15 \div 1,000 = .015$. This is also known as a banner click rate.

Pulling together an executive summary

> **Startups Tip**
> For more information on how to write a compelling executive summary, check out Startups (www.startups.co.uk/the-executive-summary.html).

This is the most important part of your plan and will form the heart of your 'elevator pitch'. Written last, this should be short and punchy – ideally one page but never more than two – and should enthuse any reader. Its primary purpose is to get an outsider – bank manager, venture capitalist, business angel or prospective partner – to want to read the rest of the plan.

The executive summary is not an attempt at summarising the whole business plan. Also, it has to tread the fine line between buzz and hype. Making unsubstantiated and unconvincing claims will be an immediate turn off, making the task of persuading your reader of the true worth of your proposal that much harder.

Executive summary: what to include . . .

- What your product/service is, why it's better or different from what is around currently, and why customers need what you plan to offer.
- What the state of competitive market environment for your product/service is like at present, and what its growth prospects are.
- How close you are to being ready to sell your product/service and what if anything remains to be done.
- Why you have the skills and expertise to start-up and run this business; who else you need to help in your business (and how you will recruit them).
- Financial projections showing how much money you need to start-up and operate until you reach cashflow break-even; if you don't have sufficient money, how much will you need to raise and what security you can offer to a lender (or shareholding for an investor).

- Milestones showing what any money raised will be used for (and when), showing measurable results.
- How you will operate your business. Sketch out the key steps from buying in any raw materials, through to selling, delivering and getting paid.
- What legal form your enterprise takes and who any other existing shareholders are (if any) with their percentage stake.
- A summarised profit and loss account showing sales income, gross profit and operating profit for the period of the business plan.

Setting out the body of the business plan

While the executive summary reveals the essence of your business proposition, the body of your business plan sets out the contents in a logical sequence. Your plan won't contain everything you have discovered from your research, every 'what if' calculation on your cashflow or every fact about your market or competitors. But it will provide readers with sufficient information to make a judgement as to whether they will give you the support you want from them.

The body of your plan will follow the order set out in your table of contents, with information as shown below.

-⟶ **Performance history:** if your business is trading include summarised financial statements, a description of the products and markets currently served and a timeline showing main stages of development since start-up. Also include details of your current auditors.

-⟶ **Strategy:** include you mission statement, vision, key objectives, competitive advantage and a brief overview of the economic, political and other forces at work in your marketplace.

-⟶ **Marketing:** information on the new/additional products/ services on offer, customers and the size of the market, competitors, proposed pricing, promotion, selling and distribution method.

- → **Operations:** with information on any processes such as manufacture, assembly, purchasing, stock holding, delivery/fulfilment and website.

- → **Financial projections:** with information on sales and cashflow for the next 12–18 months, showing how much money is needed, for what and by when. Include summarised profit and loss accounts, balance sheets and key ratios.

- → **Premises:** what space and equipment will be needed and how (if appropriate) your home will accommodate the business while staying within the law.

- → **Legal structure and ownership:** is your venture a limited company, and if so who owns the shares? Is an employee share option scheme in force? If you are trading as a limited company, name the directors, company secretary, accountants and auditors.

- → **People:** what skills and experience you have that will help you run this business; what other people will you need and where will you find them?

- → **Administrative matters:** do you have any IP on your product or service? What insurance will you need? What bookkeeping and accounting system will you use? How will you keep customer, supplier and employee records? How will performance be monitored, controlled and reported on?

- → **Professional advisors:** who you have used for help and advice on website design, search engine optimisation, tax, accounting procedures, IP, grants, market data and any other areas critical to your venture.

- → **Key risks:** what critical risks do you foresee? Include a summary of your stress tests of the revenue and payments models you are using as well as details of any insurance you will be taking out.

- → **Non-executive directors:** names, experience and relevance to your business strategy. Their terms of reference and reward structure.

All these topics are covered in this book, and by using the index and table of contents you should be able to find them quickly.

> **Startups Tip**
> For more information on what to include in the body of your business plan, check out Startups (www.startups.co.uk/what-goes-in.html).

Employing appendices

While a business plan is not a work of literature, it should read well. Anything essential that could impede a smooth flow should be consigned to an appendix and either summarised or referenced in the main body of the plan.

Items best included in an appendix include:

→ CVs of key staff

→ detailed market research studies, surveys, questionnaires and findings

→ competitors' literature, accounts and related information

→ full financial projections – balance sheets, profit and loss accounts, cashflow projections, 'what if' analysis, break-even calculations and detailed ratio analysis

→ patent and other IP currently owned or being applied for

→ website screen shots

→ literature, brochures, product specifications and designs.

Checklist

- ☑ Make sure your business plan is visually attractive when it comes to packaging.

- ☑ Consider using an appendix if you have lots of bulky information: market research, CV etc.

- ☑ Make sure you have put contact details on the plan's cover.

- ☑ Think about any words your readers may not understand and consider including a glossary.

- ☑ Take steps to protect your plan using a non-disclosure agreement.

Conclusion

G iven all the other tasks involved in starting up in business, it's hardly surprising many entrepreneurs give writing a business plan a miss. More exciting things to do than sitting down hammering out words and charts are not hard to find. Searching out premises, negotiating with suppliers, getting a website up and running or going to an exhibition to check out competitors all sound like more important tasks for an entrepreneur to fill their days (and nights) with. Hopefully by now you are convinced of the merits of taking the time to research and write up a great business plan and have the skills and knowledge to do so.

Everything you need to write a business plan is here in the book. Throughout the chapters there are powerful business planning tools and up-to-the-minute advice on all the myriad of rules and regulations that your plan has to accommodate. Hopefully your research will uncover many of the pitfalls that beset every entrepreneur. Keep in mind what Alfred Sheinwold, the international bridge player, had to say on this subject: "Learn all you can from the mistakes of others. You won't have time to make them all yourself." With this in mind your business plan should help you chart a course to a profitable and secure future.

Appendix: Case studies

Learn from those who have gone before you! From one-time bus conductor, Simon Woodroffe, fixing on the idea for his YO! Sushi chain of restaurants following a chance remark from a Japanese acquaintance at lunch, to Nick Jenkins honing his business model for online greetings card business Moonpig while on an MBA at Cranfield School of Management, these people have been there and done it.

Read about their first-hand experiences here, and benefit from their hard-won advice and telling insights throughout the book.

Information has been supplied by the following people:

- → Edwina Dunn and Clive Humby, dunnhumby

- → Adam Balon, Jon Wright and Richard Reed, innocent

- → Nick Jenkins, Moonpig

- → Holly Tucker, Sophie Cornish, Notonthehighstreet.com

- → Mary Perkins, Specsavers

- → Simon Woodroffe, YO! Sushi

In my experience

Nick Jenkins' business idea back in 1999 was simple. He would take the bog standard greetings card that has been around since

Founders: Nick Jenkins
Company: Moonpig
Start year: 1999
Type: Online greeting card retailer

Victorian times, and create a website where customers could personalise their own humorous cards. Nick calculated that he could create a profitable business where customers bought a single personalised card, with prices starting at £2.99 plus postage. The cards would be sent out on the same day, either directly to the recipient, or to the sender to pass on to someone else. Judging from the positive reaction he had had to his own rudimentary efforts he was confident that the idea would catch on. Operating as an online business, he would also be collecting payments upfront, leading him to think that cashflow would be good.

Nick took the idea to Paperlink, a successful greeting card publishing company without an online presence, and offered them a small stake in the company if they would let the as-yet-unnamed company use their greeting card designs. Miraculously they agreed and this was enough to convince Nick that the idea he had was worth pursuing.

Nick ploughed £160,000 of his own money (from his share of a sugar trading management buy-out) into the business and raised a further £125,000 from three friends who were keen to invest in Moonpig. Immediately after registering the company in October 1999, Nick hired a website design agency to help him build and design the site, with the aim of going live by Christmas 1999. In the business's first year of trading, it distributed around 40,000 cards, and made a loss of around £1 million on sales of £90,000. The losses were mostly incurred on overheads, such as staff, printing equipment, software development and marketing.

By 2002, the economy was slowly starting to emerge from the shadows of the dotcom bust but things were still bleak. Nick had originally anticipated that the business would break-even in year three, but in fact, it took five years and six further rounds of fundraising from private investors for Moonpig to reach profitability.

By 2004, it seemed that all the hard work was finally paying off – sales were continuing to grow and the lines between loss and break-even were blurring. Sales had grown steadily from the beginning, based largely on word of mouth and referrals. As every product was unique and was branded with the Moonpig.com domain name, the more it sold the more customers it attracted. By 2005, the business was making a profit.

As well as offering personalised cards, Moonpig started creating cards that looked like spoof magazine covers, such as OK and Hello!. In 2006, as well as expanding its product base, Moonpig made the decision to expand overseas, starting with Australia. Nick says it was the logical step towards growth as the country is culturally very similar to UK with respect to card buyers.

Moonpig now accounts for over 90% of the online greetings card market and now sells more than 10 million cards a year which, if laid out end to end, would stretch from London to Moscow. In July 2011 the company was bought out by PhotoBox, a digital photo service provider for £120 million.

In my experience

dunnhumby was founded by husband and wife team Edwina Dunn and Clive Humby in 1989, at a time when the UK was plummeting into recession. Armed with a firm belief in their pioneering idea, and

Founders: Edwina Dunn and Clive Humby

Company: dunnhumby

Start year: 1989

Type: Marketing

not much else, the husband and wife team needed to convince clients of the value of customer data, as well as build data technology from scratch. They approached their employer with the idea, but were met with a cold reception.

They presented their business plan to some of their industry contacts, including Geoffrey Squire, CEO of Oracle UK at the time and an angel investor. He had been a colleague at a previous employer and was so impressed by what the two were looking to achieve that he invested £250,000 in 1990.

To get their first client, they used their existing contacts list, approaching a few with a simple explanation of what they could offer, and how it could impact on their clients' business. Within two months, they found their first client, food wholesaler Booker Cash and Carry, which operated in the business-to-business sector. The business was growing steadily, until 1994, when dunnhumby caught the eye of Tesco. An executive from the marketing department of supermarket Tesco had heard Clive speak at an industry conference, and was clearly impressed. He presented the two founders with a challenge. Tesco was trialling a loyalty scheme, the Clubcard, in nine of its stores and was interested in finding out if dunnhumby could help to measure and improve its performance. Edwina and Clive were told not to build their hopes up, however – this would be a one-off exercise as Tesco rarely used external companies.

By this time, dunnhumby had grown to around 40 people operating from a small office in Chiswick, near Edwina and Clive's house. Everyone pitched in to help prepare the analysis for Tesco, which was presented a month later to the same marketing executive – Grant Harrison. dunnhumby was analysing Tesco customer data based on what people did and did not buy in-store. Rather than sending promotional offers to all customers, data analysis enabled them to look at customers on an individual basis, identify their characteristics and buying patterns, and then target promotions and communications accordingly. The idea was to encourage repeat sales and tempt customers into buying new products that appealed to their existing preferences. In Edwina's words, the representative was 'blown away' by their work and invited dunnhumby to present it to the Tesco board, including Sir Ian MacLaurin, the supermarket's chairman. Their presentation was a rousing success.

Building on their Tesco experience, dunnhumby currently analyses data from over 350 million people in 25 countries, using this insight to improve the customer's brand experience. Kroger – Macy's – PAM – Groupe Casino – Monoprix – CBD Brazil – Almacenes Exito Columbia – Metro – Best Buy – Canadian Tire – have all taken onboard dunnhumby's central vision – the customer knows best so you have to be the best at knowing your customer. Today, dunnhumby, now a wholly owned subsidiary of Tesco, employs around 1,200 people in Europe, Asia and America with a turnover of around £300 million.

In my experience

The gradual homogenisation of the UK high street over the past few decades has created a growing culture of people keen to seek out unique commodities. Traditionally this kind of

Founders: Holly Tucker, Sophie Cornish

Company: Notonthehighstreet.com

Start year: 2006

Type: Online marketplace

fodder was only available at craft exhibitions, but in 2006 Holly Tucker and Sophie Cornish launched Notonthehighstreet.com, an online marketplace showcasing the products of more than 800 businesses.

Holly and Sophie had both run their own businesses before joining forces on the highly successful Notonthehighstreet.com. The pair met a decade earlier while working for an advertising agency and went on to set up ventures in the events and shopping sectors. Working within these industries they realised there was a wealth of quirky and distinctive retailers without an affordable and effective method of selling their products.

Most of these businesses did not have an online presence, and of the ones that did, there was virtually no e-commerce capability. These businesses were desperate for a way of reaching customers without lugging their products around the country attending really expensive trade fairs which could cost thousands to exhibit at.

Confident of the demand for the offering, the pair moved into an office in January 2006 and four months later they launched the first version of the site which, despite gaining some excellent coverage, was not without its teething problems. Some great PR coups, including several mentions in the nationals, meant there were 16,000 unique visitors to the site on launch day, but because of a technical error the e-commerce function didn't work.

Holly and Sophie had begged, borrowed and stolen from savings, friends and family to get the site live but at the end of the first year they hit a cashflow crisis. They needed funding fast so began the arduous task of pitching what investors saw as 'yet another female shopping site' to dozens of stone-faced venture capitalists. Investment eventually came in the form of Spark Ventures, early backers of Lastminute.com, and during the following year the business grew by 600%. Revenue comes in the form an initial seller fee and 23% commission on sales.

After closing a second round of funding in July 2008, the business ended the year boasting 800 sellers and a transactional turnover of £2.5 million. In 2011 a panel of expert judges including venture capitalists and angel investors compiling *The Telegraph*'s Tech Start-Up 100 list of the year's most promising young technology companies rated Notonthehighstreet.com one of the success stories. Also in 2011, the company recruited senior managers from Amazon, PayPal and Google as it prepares for international expansion. Jason Weston, previously director of UK Softlines at Amazon, has joined as its chief operating officer, Mark Hodson, previously marketing director at PayPal UK has been appointed chief marketing officer, while Maya Moufarek, a founding member of Google's EMEA emerging markets team, joined as the new director of international development. Today the company employs 65 people at its Richmond-upon-Thames headquarters and its turnover has risen from £100,000 in its first year to £15.1 million in 2011.

👤 In my experience

innocent drinks are cool. The smoothies in small plastic bottles with witty alternative labelling are the drinks to be seen with – at almost £2 per 250ml they should be too. But innocent is no passing fad,

Founders: Adam Balon, Jon Wright, Richard Reed

Company: innocent

Start year: 1999

Type: Natural foods

for it has succeeded where virtually every nutritionist has failed: making fruit fun and being healthy easy. Started in 1998 by three young friends with no sector experience or financial backing the start-up was more measured than meteoric. Richard Reed and his co-founders Adam Balon and Jon Wright had absolutely no experience in fruit or the drinks market, going from idea to reality obviously involved doing some research. They started out buying fruit and making up recipes that they thought tasted good; once they had drinks that they liked and their friends liked they knew they were on the right track.

Public approval for innocent came after the now legendary experiment at a jazz festival where the drinks were sold and people asked to place their empty cups in a 'yes' or 'no' bin to vote whether the three lads should give up their jobs and make smoothies full-time. With the 'yes' bin recording a landslide victory they quit their jobs the next day. Over that first weekend, innocent drinks made it into 50 shops and were an immediate success, with 45 wanting more.

At one point when the business stalled with sales slipping back and their European expansion soaking up cash at a rapid rate the founders, average age 28, decided that they needed some heavyweight advice and talked to Charles Dunstone, Carphone Warehouse founder and Mervyn Davies, chairman of Standard Chartered. The strong advice was to get an investor with deep pockets and ideally something else to bring to the party to augment the youthful enthusiasm of the founders. A score of unsuccessful bids for bank finance and dozens of presentations to venture capitalists drew a blank. An email round robin secured an introduction to an American business angel, who invested £2.5 million to get things off the ground.

By May 2007 a tie up with McDonald's saw innocent smoothies selling in 70 restaurants in a trial that can be seen as a crucial turning point in the company's history. To facilitate the next stage of growth, in April 2009 the innocent team accepted Coca-Cola as a minority investor in its business, paying £30 million (US$ 47 million/€34 million) for a stake of between 10% and 20%. The team chose Coca-Cola because as well as providing the funds, it can help get innocent products out to more people in more places. A year later Coca-Cola increased its stake to 58%, giving it a majority holding. innocent, with sales in excess of £100 million a year, has three-quarters of the UK smoothies market.

In my experience

Every once in a while an entrepreneur turns an industry on its head. Dame Mary Perkins is a perfect example. In 1984, she launched a business

Founders: Mary Perkins

Company: Specsavers

Start year: 1984

Type: High street opticians

that changed the face of optometry for good. We might be used to visiting showrooms to purchase glasses these days, trying on frames at our leisure until we find the perfect fit, with every item clearly priced, but back in the early 1980s this was not the case. Before Mary launched Specsavers, consumers had very little choice or control when purchasing eyewear. The once state-owned optics business was going through deregulation in the early 1980s. Under its previous ownership, opticians could not even advertise their products or services. Indeed, before Specsavers came along, when you visited an optician they'd disappear out back to find a few pairs for you to try on. But Mary had a clear vision of how opticians could operate in order to deliver better value, choice and transparency to consumers. Driven by a mission of providing affordable eye care to all, she built the company around the idea of treating others respectfully. Twenty-five years later, she still describes her billion pound international company, which she founded with her husband, Doug Perkins, as 'a family-owned business, with family values'.

She invested around £500,000 from the sale of her first business to get the fledgling Specsavers off the ground, buying equipment and sourcing products, establishing contacts and hiring staff. This investment also provided working capital to bring the business to profitability, which was achieved after just 12 months, despite the addition of four more stores in Guernsey, Swansea, Bath and Plymouth. One of the key lessons Mary had learned was the importance of setting yourself apart from the competition by establishing USPs. As a new business, there was no point in merely copying a major player — you had to offer customers something different.

She identified a number of major problems with the way opticians were doing business at the time, and came up with a proposition that she felt was far more attractive to consumers. First of all, glasses were expensive. Mary believed that she would be able to bring prices down without compromising on quality by negotiating better buying terms and selling larger volumes. For example, instead of buying from wholesalers who added a significant mark-up on their prices, she went to factories directly.

Growing the business was hard work. Mary and her husband Doug worked long hours, and balanced building a customer database and opening more practices with looking after three young children. But their hard work paid off. From just two staff working at a table-tennis table, there are now more than 500 based at Specsavers' headquarters in Guernsey and around 26,000 worldwide. The company has more than 1,390 stores across the Channel Islands, UK, Ireland, the Netherlands, Scandinavia, Spain, Australia and New Zealand. Mary believes that much of her success has been driven by the preservation of the founding culture and ideals, and a focus on giving consumers real value and choice.

In my experience

One-time bus conductor Simon Woodroffe has done pretty much everything. Now the owner of YO! Sushi is ready to go global. He left school

> Founders: Simon Woodroffe
> Company: YO! Sushi
> Start year: 1997
> Type: Japenense 'kaiten' sushi bar

at the age of 16 and spent the next three decades designing and staging concerts in London and Los Angeles, covering performers from the Moody Blues to Madness and Rod Stewart to George Michael. Events such as Live Aid also came under his operating umbrella.

The idea for Simon's first business came when he was having lunch with a Japanese man who said, "What you should do Simon is a Conveyor Belt Sushi Bar with girls in black PVC mini skirts". Simon found out there were 3,000 of them in Japan.

The £650,000 funding to start his businesses came from his life savings of £50,000 and two friends put up £100,000. The rest came from the Government Loan Guarantee scheme, a lot of expensive leasing and eventually credit from his suppliers.

The jobs Simon did before he started his own business include bus conductor, roadie, stage designer, TV rights distributor, ski bum, sports filmmaker, in that order. In his own opinion every single one of them helped him. The skills and personal characteristics that he considers essential to success in your own business include determination, realism and enthusiasm. His inspiration came from Richard Branson.

A busy man, Simon still manages to strike the right work/life balance: "I always say work work, live live. I've always done a lot but friends are a great way of keeping you in check. It's important I get on with my ex-wife, my friends, my girlfriends, it's about being happy. I always say my left shoulder is very serious and work-orientated, but with exact equal measure my right doesn't think YO! Sushi or anything else success-related is that important at all

— if one starts to weigh more than the other then I know it needs looking at."

So how does he measure personal success? Simon has had plenty of recognition from the 1998 Marketing Week Design Effectiveness Award to an OBE awarded for services to the hospitality industry in 2006. But his opinion "It's an inner feeling and a knowledge I've done things 'my way'. I'm proud to have formed all sorts of great relationships with lots of different people; but mostly that I had a dream that came true." If there was a single moment when Simon knew he's made it then it was simply opening the first YO! Sushi because it realised a dream, regardless of what happened after.

In 2012, YO! Sushi turned 15 and the group has now grown to more than 50 restaurants including those in the department stores Harvey Nichols and Selfridges, across London and now the world. YO! serves over three million customers every year. Simon continues to build new YO! businesses, and provided the seed capital and much of the design work for YOTEL, which now operates at Heathrow, Gatwick and Amsterdam airports. YOTEL also opened a 669-room site in New York just two blocks west of Times Square, in the middle of Manhattan in 2011. Simon is currently working on the development of new YO! Ventures including YO! Home and YO! Zone.